In the
Dry Season

Surviving Your Desert

A book by

RONTRELL P. EDWARDS

IN THE DRY SEASON
BY RONTRELL P. EDWARDS

Copyright © 2013 by Rontrell P. Edwards

All Rights Reserved

This book or parts thereof may not be reproduced in any form, stored in a retrieval system, or transmitted in any form by any means-electronic, mechanical, photocopy, recording, or otherwise- without prior written permission of the publisher, except as provided by United States of America copyright law.

CONTENTS

Introduction…………………………………………….5

1. The "It" Factor………………………………………7

2. What is this?………………………………………..13

3. Key to Knowledge…………………………………27

4. Once and For All…………………………………...38

5. Seasons for Reasons………………………………..41

6. Discerning the Seasons……………………………..50

7. God of Seasons……………………………………..64

8. Plain Ole' Dry………………………………………70

9. Too Close for Comfort……………………………..75

10. As God Commanded……………………………...83

11. Always Winter Never Christmas………………….93

12. Pain of Waiting…………………………………..112

13. Dry Season=Destiny……………………………..122

14. Drenched Trench………………………………...143

Dedication:

First, my thanks to God without His voice this book would not be possible.

To my mother who laid the foundation for my coming to know Christ.

To my little brothers who continue to make me proud.

And to my spiritual mother who is always pouring into my life and allows me to climb on her shoulders to catapult me into my God-given destiny.

And to everyone else who poured into me spiritually. I would not be who I am today with you!

Thank You All!!

Lastly but not least this book is dedicated to the Christians struggling in their faith. Above all else my heart for writing this book was to be the helping hand and encouragement you need to hang in there. Moses needed Aaron and Hur to hold up his hands during battle. This is my prayer that this book will help you through your greatest battles. If this book touches one life I am eternally grateful.

Luke 4:18 "The Spirit of the Lord is on me, because he has anointed me to preach good news to the poor. He has sent me to proclaim freedom for the prisoners and recovery of sight to the blind, to release the oppressed."

Introduction

It was my first year in ministry school. We were learning how to prepare messages, how to pray for people's needs, and how to become leaders by serving others. What I share in this book I have never heard preached or taught. It is through God's grace, and my life experiences that this book is being written. God supernaturally opened my eyes to receive this divine revelation. I am amazed at the insight that God has revealed to me. All Christians will or have already experienced a dry season. It is the season Christians dread the most. The dry season is one of the most difficult things to face as a Christian. The dry seasons are those seasons when God feels far away and His voice is a distant memory. It is the season we feel stuck and bland. The dry season is a season no one looks forward to. Sensing God in those seasons feels impossible. The winter times of our life are the hardest, but the most impactful. Did you know that your dry season is connected to your destiny? The way one handles a dry season is based on their understanding of what is happening. As I unveil the revelation that God has exposed to me, my prayer is for this book to have a tremendous comfort to the hearts that desire to serve God.

Chapter 1

The "IT" Factor

It was the April 2010. The reason the date is so clear to me is because it was my first year in Bible College. It may not seem like a big deal to you, but for me it was unprecedented. April 2010; however, will be a month I will never forget. Before we get to what exactly happened that day, let me take time to explain to you my life up until that point. That year (2010) was the first year I had relentlessly pursued the call of God on my life. I left my old life, home, and family to enroll in ministry school. My high school years were full of days fitting in with the crowds. I was the athlete on the school campus, and I lived up to the stereotype. My mind was focused on girls and drinking. I am a person that does everything one hundred percent. When I lived for the world, I had the same mindset. Whatever I did, I did all out. I would mask my hurts and insecurities with a lifestyle full of sin. Church was something that I didn't pay much attention to because I figured it was irrelevant. What could a book written two thousand years ago teach me? Why would I surrender my life to a

God that I felt dealt me an unfair hand in life? I looked around at my friends who all had both parents. I felt cheated and I blamed God. I was stuck between two parents who did not get along. I found myself asking where God was up to this point in my life. I felt as if church and God were irrational, especially in the twenty first century. On one Wednesday evening when I found myself unfulfilled and seeking more from life, God began to do an extraordinary work on my soul. I gave my life to God, and the story unfolds from there. Like I previously stated anything I committed to I did one hundred percent. When I lived in the world I was a radical sinner who did everything to the extreme. Nothing was different with my newly found Christian life. I was all in. Chains in my life had been broken. God was made real to me. I walked around carrying a lighter load than before. I wanted to be radical. I wanted to share my Jesus with everyone I came in contact with. I could not settle for just being a "normal" Christian. God continued to call me to a higher level. I sensed that God did not want me to be one of the pew sitting Christians that are found in so many American churches. My heart began to long for revival to spark in my generation. I wanted God to show up in other people's lives just the way he did in my life. The hunger inside of me would not allow me to settle for anything but God's best. I decided to pursue the call of God on my life by enrolling in Bible College. It was one of the most difficult things that I ever had to do because I had no idea what the outcome would be. The decision to enter into ministry school was an extreme step of faith. It was stepping into a land unfamiliar to me and my family. I am not second or third generation preacher. I am the first in my family to feel God calling them into a ministerial role. It would have been simpler if my dad would have been a pastor. I could rely on his advice and wisdom. He could teach me things to be aware of when beginning a life of ministry. I unfortunately, did not have that privilege. I had to step out of the boat in total faith just as Peter did. I did not know, however; that stepping into the unknown would land me straight in the middle of the will of God. It was amazing just a few months prior I was smoking joints and running around with all sorts of girls, but God eradicated all of my short falls and found me worthy of ministry. I was officially enrolled in Bible College. I began taking Bible courses with college professors. I began to have one on one time with pastors. The bible began to become relevant to me. The scriptures the preachers used in their sermons began to make sense to me. I began to pray daily. In those prayer times, I felt God's tangible presence.

I was like a kid in a candy store. I had never been more excited in my life. I made a decision to follow God, and the excitement of serving Jesus overwhelmed me. I had no idea that the Christian life could feel this way. The feelings that I felt were uncontainable. This excitement compelled me to go out and tell the world. I would witness to random people and saw countless of backslidden Christians repent with teary eyes. On one occasion, a man who had not attended church for years recommitted his life to Jesus at a gas station. On another occasion, my classmates and I were witnessing at Mardi Gras in the middle of Bourbon street. This was a scene to witness folks. People from all over the world flood New Orleans to take part of the unmentionable things that take place at Mardi Gras. One, in their rational mind, would think that this would be the last place sinners would get saved. You would be wrong. As five to six hundred Bible College students rushed the street of Bourbon with worship in their mouth, God began to save people in the midst of everything that was going on. I had the chance to witness to a young man who had come to wits end. As I began to share with him the gospel, this young man took 4-5 crack rocks out of his pocket and began to admittedly crush them with the soles of his feet. As he continued this bold move out of his mouth rang

"I am done living like this." These countless supernatural encounters became normal in my life. I had no idea the Christian life was this exuberating. My idea of a Christian was a two-talking hypocrite that lived an uneventful life. I thought Christians were either boring or judgmental. The way I viewed a Christian was someone who locked themselves away with other Christians because they were too good for anyone else. Many non-Christians toady feel the same way I once did. The church needs to stop being inclusive to only church people. If we only witness to church people then church people will only fill the church. Jesus called us to go out into the world. Get off your pew and do something. Now that I got that off of my chest, let's get back to the topic at hand. My ideologies about the Christian life had been exposed and put to rest. This had been the most eventful time in my life. Mind you athletes in high school have plenty eventful years, but those days could not measure up to the sense of fulfillment that I had found myself in. The reason I felt so fulfilled was because I found my calling in life. You will never find a sense of peace with yourself until you find out why God placed you on this earth. Finding that reason is only the first stage. The next is to pursue that call. Many people strive to chase monetary gain and find out late in life after the big house, big car, and big bank account that they are still unfulfilled. You can reference the countless lottery winners who find themselves in worst positions now than before the winnings. You will never feel a sense of peace until you find your purpose here on Earth. I found my purpose in life. I tasted and saw glimpses of what God wanted to accomplish in my life. God showed me that my life was to be dedicated to him. In return God would give me the grace to turn a generation's focus on the soon coming king. I was ecstatic. I had never felt this way before. My spirit man was thriving not just surviving. I was feeding my soul and had a true relationship with God. If you do not know what this feeling is like, you are missing out. We are created to have relationship with Our Creator. "Though the outward man dies the inward man is renewed day by day." God was giving me this sense of renewal. All my past faults and failures had no place in my life any longer. God allowed me to start over. My life had purpose and meaning. The rest of my life could not have come quickly enough. I felt as if I wasted enough of my life pursuing things that did not matter. I just wanted to lie at the feet of Jesus and submit to his will. I was on a spiritual high when all of a sudden "it" came out of nowhere.

2
What Is This?

After months of being on a spiritual high and seeing God's work in my life and the lives of people around me, something changed. I wasn't able to put my finger on it, but something about my spiritual walk felt different. It was April 2010. The school year was coming to an end. Classes were winding down and final exams were being studied for. The ministry team that traveled began wrapping up their traveling schedule. My classmates were excited because in a few weeks, they would be returning home for the summer. This would be the first time they would spend an extended period of time around their families. All my classmates wanted to show their families how much they had changed. Most of my classmates had stories similar to me. Most of us had no idea how to be an on fire Christian before Bible College. After our first year, we all felt as though we could shake the world. During those months, we developed lifelong spiritual disciplines. We would soon bring those disciplines home with us for the summer. Our families would get to see how much we had grown spiritually. Some had grown so much that they were literally different people than when they had started. While everyone else laughed, joked, and talked about what they were planning for the summer; I could not join in on the conversations. My classmates would have conversations about what God was sharing to them in their private prayer lives. Usually I would join in on the conversation and tell a testimony about what God was sharing to me. I couldn't join in on those conversations. I had to settle for listening to them share vividly about their God moments. Something was different. My worship experience was different. I did not sense the tangible presence of God that I was accustomed to. When I prayed, I felt like my prayers were bouncing off the walls and coming back to me. When I read the bible, it felt as if it was just mere words on a page. For the first time, I felt like God had abandoned me. I had never experienced this before. What happened to the excitement and all the revelation that God had been giving me? Why all of a sudden had God stop speaking to me. Why couldn't I feel his presence anymore? I could only ask myself, "What is this?" All around I saw my classmates excited and talking about the things God was doing in their lives. Watching them with such joy and passion only made me question more what happened to my relationship with God. Listening to classmates reminded me of the great times I had with God. I didn't understand what was going on. I was still a new Christian, but I found myself asking where are you God? I attributed my feeling of emptiness and abandonment to me shifting my focus from God to the up and coming summer. I felt that I had been focused on returning home, playing with my younger brothers, helping out with my home youth ministry, and relaxing from school work. I figured the next day would be better because I would return my focus on God rather than the summer. I was wrong. The days turned into weeks, and still I could not find God. I witnessed classmates crying in the altars at church, jumping during worship, and talking about scriptures that spoke to their hearts. I witnessed their relationship with God and wondered what was going on with me. I remember thinking this is not what I signed up for. The pain of not understanding what was going on was unbearable. I couldn't take missing God. I remember saying to myself, if this is a part of being a Christian then I don't want any part of it. I contemplated whether or not I should run away and never look back. Thoughts popped up in my head telling me that I should go back to my old life. Whatever was going on with me was making me miserable. I did not know it at the time, but I had entered my first dry season.

No Where To Be Found?

> *"When the people saw that Moses was so long in coming down from the mountain, they gathered around Aaron and said. Come; make us gods who will go before us." Exodus 32:1*

The Israelites could attest to what it feels like to enter into a dry season or wilderness. The Israelites had been in bondage for 400 years. Pharaoh after Pharaoh continued to enslave the Israelites in Egypt. God raised up a man by the name of Moses to lead his people out of Egyptian captivity. The beginning stages of the Israelites journey with God were full of worship and songs. God performed great miracles in the sights of the Israelites. Rods became serpents, rivers became blood, and the Egyptian cattle suddenly dying were only a few of the miracles God performed while insisting that Pharaoh let his people go. This reminds me of the persistence God showed toward me. God continued to call and perform miracles in my life in order to set me free from my sin. Just as the

Israelites, God will do the same for you. You cannot out run God. There is nowhere that you can go that is off limits to God. The prodigal son in the book of Luke found himself in the pig's pen of life, but still the Father was looking a long way off for him. After the countless miracles, God instructed the Israelites in Exodus 19 to stop in the Sinai desert. The desert always represents barren and dry lands. It represents a process of God wanting to develop and take you to a better place. The desert always seems to be correlated with isolation. As humans one of the hardest things we face is loneliness. We try to fill those empty places in our lives with temporary solutions like money, spouses, and work; but none of those things are permanent fixes. God is the only thing that can fill that void. Once God has become real to you and you witness the countless miracles that He has done in pursuit of you, it is hard being in a desert place where you can't find him. The dry season will make you feel as if you are isolated and by yourself. The desert represents those seasons in your life where you just feel dry. The Israelites entered into their first dry season. Up until this point, God had been with the Israelites. The Israelites undeniably felt the Lord's protection and presence as they walked through the Red Sea. Unquestionably, the Israelites heard the Lord's voice through his servant Moses. They were experiencing the same joy and excitement that I had become accustomed to. I could sing songs to God all day. God's wonders had me speechless. This is the same way I picture the Israelites. After witnessing countless miracles, the Israelites undoubtedly found themselves feeling near and close to God. No doubt their spirits were erupting from the joy that comes with knowing that God has your back. Suddenly, the Israelites found themselves in a dry, desert land. The Israelites hadn't experienced this before. They had grown accustomed to hearing Moses speak for God, but Moses was on top of a mountain. They had grown used to seeing great miraculous signs from heaven, but there were no signs following them at the time. The Israelites were used to moving forward, but they find themselves at a standstill in the desert of Sinai. What makes the matter worst is while they were in the valley of the desert; they had to witness Moses on his mountaintop. It must have been hard witnessing Moses experiencing the very tangible presence of God while they were dry and stuck. Being in a dry season is hard all by itself, but what makes it worst is being in a dry place and having to witness someone else on their mountaintop. You don't have anything against that person who is on the mountaintop. You just question your own spirituality and how you long for the same experience. Watching my classmates tell testimony after testimony on God's goodness was extremely difficult. It wasn't difficult because I was unhappy for my classmates. Deep in my heart I was thrilled that I was involved with friends that could hear and experience God. The part that made it difficult was I wanted that experience. I wanted to be on the mountaintop. I wanted to join in on the conversations about what God was doing in my life. When I looked at their lives, it made me long more for what I did not have at the time. While Moses is on the mountaintop, the Israelites were in the desert having to witness from a distance the glory cloud that covered the mountain. The Bible says that *"When the people saw that Moses was so long in coming down from the mountain, they gathered around Aaron and said. Come; make us gods who will go before us."* The Israelites asked something strange from Aaron. The Israelites asked Aaron to make them gods that will go before them. Wait a minute can you repeat that! This would be the point in the story that I would ask the Israelites (politely of course), WHAT ARE YOU SMOKING? The Israelites wanted to make gods that went before them. Why would they want to do that? Why would they want to replace the God that just split the Red Sea before their very eyes? Did not God do enough for them? Wouldn't every person with common sense remember that God just saved them from the Egyptians? Did the Israelites have short term memory lost? Why would they need another god? This is the very question I asked while reading this passage. If you have ever been in a dry desert place, the answer is simple. The Israelites find themselves in desert place, and every time you are in a desert place it feels as though God has abandoned you. The Israelites did not want to replace God just because they needed something to do. The Israelites did not forget that God had just performed major signs and wonders. What the Israelites struggled with was they could not find God. The Israelites felt as if God left them, so they wanted to take matters into their own hands. Dry Seasons feel as though God has walked away from your side. The Israelites looked for God and could not find him, so they decided to take matters into their own hands. We look back and say that the Israelites were foolish for thinking that God had left them. We say the Israelites were foolish for wanting to take matters into their own hands, but what we fail to realize is that we do the same things today. If we pray about that new job opening and God doesn't answer our prayers on our schedule, we do what we feel is best and find out three years down the road the job wasn't what we wanted or expected. What about praying about that man or woman we should marry and God delays an answer in a time we deem appropriate? Five years down the road, we find out that the man or woman we dated is not the same man or woman we married. The Israelites found themselves in a dry season and felt as if God had left them. They figured that they needed to create gods because they did not know where God had gone.

∎∎∎∎∎∎∎

Another interesting fact about this story is what the Israelites decided to make their god with. The Israelites went to Aaron requesting him to make a new god because the other God was nowhere to be found. Aaron being the seeker sensitive pastor he was, agreed to do as the people wanted instead of standing on the word of God. Aaron commands the Israelites to take off all their jewelry, and Aaron makes a calf out of their gold. I have two questions to present to you. Where did the Israelites get their jewelry, and where did Aaron get the idea to make a calf? The answer to the first question is found in Exodus 12:35. Moses asked Pharaoh to let his people go. Pharaoh stubbornly declined God's offer.

God to prove his point to Pharaoh sends several different signs and plagues on the Egyptians. The last plague was the killing of all the firstborns whose household was not covered by blood. After this last and horrible plague, the Egyptians wanted to get rid of the Israelites anyway they could. On the way out of Egypt, the Egyptians loaded the Israelites with all of their jewelry. The Israelites received both gold and silver from the Egyptians as they left Egypt. This was the jewelry the Israelites used to make the golden calf. This is an illustration of how some can use the gifts of the Spirit as tools to exalt idols. Anything not named God and is worshiped is an idol. Pastors that accept the glory for miracles the Spirit manifest are becoming the golden calf the Israelites worship. When I minister and the Spirit does an amazing work, I am quick to turn the people's attention to Jesus. I will not be found in competition with the Holy Spirit. God gave the Israelites departing gifts by putting on the Egyptians heart to give away their jewelry, and the Israelites turn those gifts into gods. Never get into the business of seeking the miracle without seeking the miracle worker. Never set your sight on the blessing without wanting a relationship with the Blesser. Seeking and pursuing signs and wonders without wanting the God who performs the wonder becomes idolatry. When you worship the gift more than the God who gave the gift, you are doing the same as the Israelites. You are erecting the golden calf with the gifts of the Spirit. The gifts of the Spirit aren't meant to bring glory to man, but rather to Jesus, but again that's another book for another day. The second question is relevant to what we are dealing with today. Where did Aaron get the idea to create a calf? Where had he seen this before? Out of all things he could have made my make a calf? It is well known in history that the Egyptians worshiped a god in the resemblance of a calf or ox. The Israelites had been in bondage to the Egyptians more than 400 years, it is more than likely they had witnessed the sacrifices made to the different Egyptian gods. The Israelites find themselves in a dry desert place, and they want to return to their old life. By Aaron building the golden calf, it shows his heart. Aaron's heart wants to turn back to his old life. The Israelites had been in Egyptian captivity for 400 years. The old life represents a life of familiarity. The Israelites knew where their next meal was going to come from in Egypt. The Israelites knew where they were going to sleep in Egypt. Aaron's heart wanted to go back to the familiar lifestyle. Even though the Israelites were in bondage, their familiarity with their previous lifestyle brought comfort. During the uncomfortable dry season, the Israelites sought the only comfort they knew which was to return to their bondage. The Israelites find themselves in a dry place. They have never been in this situation before, and their God cannot be found. During the dry season, the easy thing to do is go back to your old lifestyle. Dry seasons are tough. The last sentence was an understatement. Dry seasons will make you question why you decided to pursue God in the first place. Here the Israelites are in the same circumstances. They find themselves wanting to return to the same habits that they practiced before God set them free. If you haven't counted the cost dry seasons will make you count the cost. I was finding this out in my own life.

3

Key to Knowledge

> *""Woe to you experts in the law, because you have taken away the key to knowledge. You yourselves have not entered, and you have hindered those who were entering." Luke 11:52*

Let's fast forward to two years later in my Bible college life. It was my third year in ministry school, and my first ever dry season was a distant memory. I still did not label it a dry season. When I thought about what I experienced toward the end of my first year, I figured I was being emotional at the time. I assumed that it wasn't as bad as my mind made it out to be at the time. The following year which would be my second year in Bible College, I had a short time in the middle of April where I felt as if God abandoned me. However, the feeling second year was nothing compared to my experience first year. Second year came and went, and I was still growing rapidly with God. After my second year, I find myself in my third year of Bible College. In my third year, I was taking extremely difficult classes, but getting use to life in ministry. Praying to God and reading my Bible had become spiritual habits. Hearing the voice of God was something I prided myself on. The three years of ministry allowed me to build a strong healthy relationship with my Father, and hearing his voice had become second nature. People ask me all the time how to decipher whether God is speaking to them or not. It is a hard question to answer, but my reply usually upsets the ones who ask it. Jesus said "My sheep hear my voice, and I know them and they know me." Jesus says that his sheep hear his voice. The implication is that the sheep recognize the voice when they hear it, and know that Jesus is the one speaking. Jesus right after says his sheep know him. There is a difference between knowing someone and knowing about someone. I know my best friends. It is crucial as a Christian, especially as a minister to have good trustworthy friends. I know my best friends. If someone comes to me and tells me something one of my best friends says, I would know right away if my best friend said it or not. This is knowing a person. When you know their heart, before they ever say a word to you is knowing a person. Growing up I loved being outside. I loved playing all the kid games like hide and go seek, tag and all the other outdoor's games. You haven't lived unless you've played those games. I would go outside and play with all my neighbors. I would get so caught up in having fun that I would lose focus of my surroundings. My mom had a rule that we could play outside and have fun, but when the street lights came on, it was time for me to go inside. I'm a competitive human being and when I'm focused everything else is obsolete. I remember one day, I was at a neighbor's house playing basketball. Of course I was winning, but that was needless to say. In all of my winning ways, I had not realized that the street lights had come on. I remember being two points away from officially winning the game, and all of a sudden a voice from down the street calls my name, "Rontrell, Rontrell." At that point, I stopped in the middle of the basketball game and looked directly up to see the street lights shining "O" so brightly. I knew exactly who's the voice was that called my name even though I didn't turn to see their face. I knew exactly what that voice wanted even though they only called my name. The voice that was calling my name was my mom, and she wanted to let me know that it was time to come inside because the street lights had come on. How did I know it was my mom calling, and how did I know what she wanted? The reason I knew my mom's voice was simple I had relationship with her every day of the twelve years I was alive. I heard her voice every day for twelve years. Hearing her voice had become second nature. When we hear a person's voice constantly when begin to understand their heart. We begin to form relationships. My mom and I had twelve years together where she would speak I would understand exactly what she wanted and why. I knew what she wanted even though she did not say, because I knew her heart. The same can be said with God. You get to a place where you have been in relationship with God and hearing his voice just becomes second nature. Once relationship is built, his heart then becomes revealed. When you're somewhere you're not supposed to be, He could just speak your name and you know what He wants. You could be doing something you're not supposed to be, and He could just say your name. You know instantly what God is wanting. When I tell people I do not have a textbook, algebraic equation to knowing God's voice; they look at me strange. When I tell them you "just know," they get upset because they are looking for an ABC answer. The true answer is his sheep recognize his voice, and his voice usually goes against whatever the flesh wants. When you are in a grocery store and there is a voice telling you to go pray for the lady in a wheelchair, and your flesh rises up and says that you will laughed at, the voice telling you to pray was probably God. First off, the devil doesn't want you praying for anyone, and secondly your flesh is contrary to God. When your flesh rises up it should be a red flag that maybe this is the voice of God. One of the biggest mistakes the church has made is thinking that knowing God's word is the same as knowing God's voice. This is not the case. One day while reading the Bible I came across Luke 11:52 which says ""*Woe to you experts in the law, because you have taken away the key to knowledge. You yourselves have not entered, and you have hindered those who were entering."* The Spirit of the Lord began to speak to me about the key of knowledge. The Holy Spirit told me that the key to knowledge is wisdom. Knowledge is only as good as the wisdom that comes along with it. Knowledge is the tool, but without wisdom on how to use the tool the tool is worthless. If you have a tool and do not have the wisdom on when to use the tool, the tool is worthless. Knowledge is God's Word and the key to God's word is his voice. If you have a tool with no wisdom, the tool is good for nothing. If you do not understand how to use the tool, the tool becomes misused. For example, if I have a garden hose which represents knowledge, but I don't have the wisdom on how to use the garden hose plants die. If I have a gun which represents knowledge, the gun can be used to feed and protect a family. The gun in the hands of a person without wisdom can also harm and kill. What determines whether the gun is used for good or bad? The wisdom of the person holding the gun determines the gun's use. If the person holding the gun does not have the wisdom to operate the safety trigger, to understand that they should not point the gun at anyone, and they should keep it away from toddlers; someone will eventually get hurt. The same gun can be used for good or evil. What cause the tool to be used for evil? The wisdom of the person holding the tool determines the tools use. The Holy Spirit began to speak to me about how the Word of God is the tool (knowledge), and the key to the tool is wisdom (God's voice.) Wisdom is the voice of God. God's word and His voice go hand in hand. In order to truly use God's word effectively, we need to hear his voice. Proverbs 15:23 says "How good is a word spoken in due season" (KJV). The assumption of the verse is not every word is a right now word. Not every word is correct for that time. You can quote someone a scripture and be judged by God because the word was out of timing. Well how do you know the correct time to release the word? The answer is by hearing God's voice. Here is a prime example of someone using the word of God without hearing God's voice. I was having a conversation with a young man one day over lunch. I had met the young man at youth event. The guy told me a little about his story, but because I had responsibility at the event I could not talk very long. Because of that, the young man wanted to have lunch with me the following day. I agreed to have lunch with him. From the time we got in the car to the time we sat down with our food, the man quoted scripture after scripture to me. It seemed like every subject matter the guy would quote scripture as if he wanted to prove something to me. I would purposefully try to change subjects. The man continued to quote scripture to me. Everything that I would say the guy reverted to scripture. Even things that had nothing to do with spiritual matters, the guy would just find a way to revert them back to scripture. It became very aggravating because I would intentionally bring up random topics to see if the guy would continue to quote scripture. I then became angry and frustrated. Not because he was quoting scripture, but because he had an alternative motive and I couldn't put my finger on what he was trying to prove. After struggling with my feeling for a while, I heard God speak to me, and he told me that the guy had unrighteous intentions. The guy was using God's holy word for ungodly purposes. He wanted to argue with me. After God spoke such a strong word to me, I immediately told the man judgment would come to him, if he continued to pervert the Word of God for ungodly purposes. I told him the Word of God is a sword and if you use that sword without wisdom someone will get hurt. I told him it is good to know scripture, but if you know scripture without knowing his voice the young man was no different than the atheists who quote scripture perverting the Word of God in order to prove they can debate Christians. After I released the word God gave me, the guy stood dumbfounded. He then began to tell me how he was brought up in church, but was backslidden. He said he made a bet with his college buddies that he could win a debate with a Bible College student. His goal was to show his college friends that he could deceive me into thinking he was a Christian because of the multitude of scriptures he used. In order to prove to his friends that he had pulled one over on me, he was recording the whole conversation on his cell phone. He was using the Word of God without wisdom. Using anything without wisdom can be dangerous. The rest of the conversation the guy did not quote another scripture. The difference between Jesus' sheep and the atheists who quote scriptures is that Jesus' sheep know his voice. Anyone with a strong memory can memorize scripture and quote it. The difference between those people and Christians is that Christians have the Holy Spirit who guides and teaches us how to use those scriptures. See the atheist that memorize scripture have the tool, but they don't have the wisdom that tells the how to use the tool. The church has failed in the same way. Instead of using the double edged sword to fight the enemy, we use it to cut each other. We want to prove that we know more scripture than the next person. Why do you think there are so many denominations? Because one person thought they knew more scripture than the next person. If the church would ever get to the place where they are not in competition with how much scripture they know, but rely on the voice of God on how to use those scriptures, the devil and his army would not know what to do with themselves. The key to knowledge is wisdom. Knowledge is knowing scripture. Wisdom is the voice of the Lord. God's voice tells you how to use God's word, so that you never misuse the powerful tool.

Chapter 4
Once and For All

The third year of Bible College was going smoothly. I was still learning ministry keys. I was learning how to allow the Holy Spirit to operate throughout services. I was still developing the gifts that God had placed inside of me. All was going well when all of a sudden, "It" was back. The feeling of dryness and missing God crept up on me. I was fine the day before. Prayer that particular morning did not feel the same. Reading my Bible did not have the same feeling as if I was reading God's word. This time I did not panic because I had gone through this in the past two years. I started questioning what the feeling was and what caused it. I did not assume I was being emotional this time because guys are not that emotional. Women on the other hand are just strange creatures. Instead of pretending as if the uncomfortable feeling did not exist, I started investigating. My investigation had not yielded any results. It was three weeks later, and the dryness was still evident. I still had not uncovered what it was that I was dealing with. One particular day my classmates and I were informed we had a meeting to go to. Come to find out, we had a guess speaker who wanted to speak to the students and the staff at the church. The woman spoke some really profound thoughts. She spoke for nearly two hours. With that said I do not remember everything that she stated that morning, but there was one thing that she said that I will never forget. During her message to the staff and my classmates, she made the statement, "I do not believe in dry seasons." When those words left her mouth and entered my heart, I had a light bulb moment. I realized what it was that I was experiencing. I was experiencing a dry season. I wish my light bulb moment would have brought with it with more clarity but I was glad to put what I felt in words. I hadn't heard much about dry seasons up to this point in my life. When the lady said dry season, it was almost as if I knew that was what I was experiencing. The woman's statement; however, threw a wrench in my thinking. She said that there was no such thing as dry seasons. This statement made me question everything. If there were no dry seasons, what had I been experiencing for the last three Aprils? What made this lady come to the conclusion that there were no dry seasons? After the meeting, these thoughts rang in my head all day. I wrote that statement down on a sheet of paper. I was determined that when I returned home I was going to solve my questions once and for all. When I returned home, the first thing I did was open my Bible. I studied Scripture to find out whether there was anything related to a dry season. It was through this study that God revealed the content of this book. That day altered my perspectives on my spiritual life forever. God gave me revelation about what the dry season was and what happens during the dry season.

5

Seasons for Reasons

"As long as the earth endures, seedtime and harvest, cold and heat, summer and winter, day and night will never cease." Genesis 8:22

When I take the time to really admire God's handiwork which we call nature, I always find myself awestruck at His creativity. I must admit that through the busyness of life, I sometimes take for granted the little things that God has done. If you take the time to rethink the Genesis account of how God called and used nothing to make the world, we should all stand amazed every time. God's creativity is one of his many characteristics. God has given man a large portion of this same creativity. God is the artist, and we are his artwork. The artwork always shows characteristics of the artist. The Bible says it this way "we are made in the image and likeness of God." When Michelangelo sculpted David, a part of Michelangelo will always remain in the sculpture. It was from

Michelangelo's perspective. The artwork always holds characteristics of the artist. The same creativity that God used to create the world, he has given us the same ability. The ability to call things that are not as though they are. God has labeled this creativity faith. In Hebrews eleven, it gives a characteristic of faith. Hebrews eleven says, "Now faith is being sure of what we hope for and certain of what we do not see." Some people argue that this is the definition of faith, but to limit faith to those two sentences is limiting the power of faith. The author of Hebrews is not trying to define faith here but rather give a characteristic of faith. It would be the same as if I said the bike is red. Red is not the definition of the bike, but it is a characteristic of the bike. Faith is so much more than hoping for something. Faith is the spiritual currency that God operates. The good news about God is that he is not a loan shark looking for the biggest bank account. Jesus said, "If you have faith as a muster seed." Even the tiniest of faith moves God because faith is the heart depending on God. When we combine our faith with obedience, Heavens move and earthly kingdoms are destroyed. When our faith meets our obedience, we begin to see Heaven invade earth. The creation account teaches us that we can call the nothings and make them something. When we look at a person struggling with their health and we see no healing, we can call health even though there seems to be no health. God looked at nothing and made water even though there was no water. We can look into a situation where there is depression and see no peace, we can release peace. This is the creation that God has given us. This creativity is also known as faith.

■■■■■■■■

When I look up and see the sun shine or when I take vacations to the beach, the majesty of God is magnified in my heart. In the beginning, God spoke a simple word "let there be." God spoke to waves and told them to begin to splash along the shore. Thousands of years ago God spoke a word for the sun to begin to rise and shine. This is amazing and shows an astonishing truth about the word of God. The word of God is powerful. All those years ago, God spoke a word for the waves to splash along the shore, and today they are still splashing. God spoke a word in the beginning that the sun should shine, and the sun is still shinning. God's word is powerful. When we find ourselves in a time a trouble, just ask God to speak. We often times try to maneuver and manipulate the situation ourselves. Sometimes all we need is God to speak a word. God's word in the beginning is still being felt today. God's word transcends time and generations. God's word has a lasting effect. In the beginning, God spoke; and the word is still relevant today.

I love to read the creation account because it is the beginning of God's dealing with man. There is so much revelation to be gained from the creation account because God gives the manuscript of what he desires from man. I haven't held many jobs because I played sports year around, but the first job I had was changing tires and oil on cars. I had no idea what I was doing when I applied for the job. I just wanted a paycheck. When I got hired, the first thing that I was required to do was sit at a computer. I did not change a tire nor did I change the oil in a car. The first thing I was required to do was sit at a computer and read all of the manuscripts of what the job expected me to do. It taught me about the different tires and how to tell them apart. It taught me the different weights of oil. It taught me how much air to put in certain tires. The job taught me what to do before I was required to do it. I stayed in the company's office completing classwork that proved I knew the principles of how to change a tire and how to change oil. The company did not assume that I knew the rules and principles of oil changing. The company did not wait until I messed up the oil in someone's car to explain the rules of changing oil, but rather the first thing they did was teach me the fundamentals of what they expected. This is what all of Genesis and the creation account does. God operates the same way. God gives us the principals and patterns in the beginning before we mess up. This is the reason I love the book of Genesis. God set up principles in the beginning that teach us what he expects from us throughout eternity. For example, there is a principle that God teaches about raising kids even before Adam and Eve had Cain and Able. God said that every seed shall produce after its own kind. God lays out a principle that every seed shall produce after its own kind. If you do not know what this means, it simply means that if you plant an apple seed an orange tree will not sprout up. It means if you plant an apple seed you will reap an apple tree. Do not expect pears when you plant apples .You may be asking what that has to do with raising kids. It has everything to do with raising kids. Parents who live by the rule do as I say and not as I do, become upset when their kids are caught doing things that they witness the parents doing. We allow a generation of kids to listen to music that glorifies sex, drugs, and violence. At the same time, we wonder why we have a generation that grows up addicted and violent. The principle remains till this day every seed will produce after its own kind. If seeds of violence, self-gratification, drugs, and rebellion are being sown into our kids' lives how can we expect them to do anything different? It would be the same as if we planted an apple tree and expected an orange tree to sprout up. When seeds of sin are planted, sin will sprout up, but the same happens when seeds of righteousness are planted. If we plant the word of God in our kid's heart, those seeds will bear fruit. Instead of having a generation of strung out kids, we would have a generation of on fire, Jesus freaks that would carry the presence of God everywhere they went. It is these kinds of principles that are flooded in the book of Genesis. God lays out the blueprints in the beginning that carries throughout eternity. The book of Genesis is rich in revelation.

When God created nature and the earth, I do not believe that he did it because he had nothing better to do. I believe everything God does is for a reason. I believe God speaks to us through his nature. Paul says, "For since the creation of the world God's invisible qualities--his eternal power and divine nature--have been clearly seen, being understood from what has been made, so that men are without excuse." Paul is saying that the visible qualities that God creates points toward spiritual qualities and principles that God is trying to show us. The Bible says that God speaks through his creation. Everything in the physical points toward the spiritual. Can I further prove it to you? God gives Moses extensive instructions on how he wants the tabernacle built. God goes through uncountable directions on what he wants, where he wants it, and how he wants it. We later find out in the book of Hebrews that God gave those extensive instructions because there was an original tabernacle in heaven. God gave Moses the blueprints in order for the copy to be a replica of the original located in heaven. The original tabernacle is in heaven, and God gives Moses instructions to make a shadow of the original here on Earth. The copy of the tabernacle here on earth points toward a tabernacle that sits in Heaven.

Going along with these same thoughts of the physical qualities in nature pointing to spiritual truths, God gives us physical seasons. God says "As long as the earth endures, seedtime and harvest, cold and heat, summer and winter, day and night will never cease." God sets up the principle of seasons here with his word. He says that seasons will always exist as long as the earth endures. What does this point to in the spiritual? Why did God find it important to set up seasons? What was God's motive in arranging and setting up seasons? The answers to these questions are simple. God wanted the physical changes of the seasons to point to the seasons that his children would go through in the spiritual.

6
Discerning the Seasons

The Pharisees and Sadducees came to Jesus and tested him by asking him to show them a sign from heaven.² He replied, "When evening comes, you say, 'It will be fair weather, for the sky is red,' ³ and in the morning, 'Today it will be stormy, for the sky is red and overcast.' You know how to interpret the appearance of the sky, but you cannot interpret the season of the time ⁴ A wicked and adulterous generation looks for a sign, but none will be given it except the sign of Jonah." Jesus then left them and went away. Matthew 16:1

The natural physical seasons are visible evidences that point to the spiritual seasons that happen throughout a Christian's life. Our lives are seasons. Our lives are filled with growth and down time. Everyone loves the growth. Everyone loves to see things blossom, but not everyone is a fan of the dry times. When they can't see growth and they feel at a standstill, people regularly bail out when the dry times come for a couple of reasons. One reason that so many people desert God is because they haven't counted the cost. Isn't it coincidental that people desert God when they think that God has deserted them? This is just evidence that proves to us all that hurt people hurt people and rejected people reject. These people are doing the same thing to God that they accuse God of doing. They are upset at God because they think that He has left them. Instead of searching for God, they are guilty of doing what they thought God did. We all know the Bible teaches us that God never leaves us, but in the dry times in sometimes feels that way. People bail out in the dry times because they have not counted the cost, and they operate off of their emotions. These are the same people that we must be cautious of. People who make decisions based off of their feelings are the people who are easily deceived because their emotions dictate their lives. Emotions are very real. It is not all the time that I walk around feeling like I'm the righteousness of Christ. It is not often that I feel like a child of the King, but my emotions do not dictate my life. The word of God dictates my life. The word of God has precedents over my emotions. The word says that I'm the head and not the tail. The Word of God says I'm above and not beneath. The Bible says that I'm blessed and highly favored. God has called me His heir. When my emotions try to tell me I'm defeated, I stand on the Word of God to dictate who I am. In the dry seasons, we feel lonely. A lot of people listen to the feelings of loneliness and ditch God altogether. When we face dry seasons in our lives, we must realize that the Word of God says that He is always there even when we may not feel him. Another reason many people desert God during their dry season is because they do not fully understand the concept of seasons. When you are experiencing growth and fruit and suddenly you feel dry, it can become devastating. One must remember that seasons change. Seasons are not permanent. We cling to those words when talking about our dry season. We love to know that our dry seasons are not permanent, but the same thing applies to our seasons of growth. An important key to not becoming frustrated in your dry season is to discern the season that you are currently in. The Pharisees and Sadducees were the religious group of Jesus' day. They were highly educated. They knew the scripture front and back. They could quote from any Old Testament passage. The Pharisees and Sadducees prided themselves on knowing scripture. They would walk around with their chest stuck out like a peacock because of their "religious status." Everyone else was mere peasants in the minds of the religious leaders. The Pharisees and Sadducees would pray a prayer with lengthy words in order to impress men. They would fast for days at a time and walk around so everyone would know they were fasting. The rest of the community looked to them as the standard of serving God. The community thought that the Pharisees and Sadducees were the pinnacle of how one should serve God. The community could only aspire to be as holy as the Pharisees and Sadducees. While the religious leaders were walking around with their necks stiffened and their noses turned up on everyone else, a thirty year old man comes onto the scene. Jesus from Nazareth begins to question the Pharisees' heart. Jesus of Nazareth begins to inquire the Sadducees motives. Jesus didn't look at their fast, but Jesus questioned why they fasted. Jesus wanted to know their heart. Did they fast to be known be men or to be known in Heaven? Jesus wasn't impressed with the Pharisees' long prayers. Jesus wanted to know why they prayed. Did they pray to impress men or did they pray to shake Heaven? Jesus can ask the same question to people today. When we pray in front of people are we doing it so people can say how well you prayed, or are we trying to reach the Father on behalf of our needs? Jesus chastised the very people everyone else wanted to be like. People were drawn to the authority that this Jesus spoke with. How could a Galilean go toe to toe with the Pharisees and

Sadducees? Of course, the religious leaders were outraged at the momentum Jesus was gaining in the people's hearts. They began to question Jesus in order to trap him. On one occasion, The Pharisees and Sadducees wanted Jesus to show them a sign. Jesus hearing their request seems to ignore it at first. Rather than Jesus answering their question directly, he immediately turned their attention to the weather. Jesus begins to speak to them about seasons. Jesus asked how was it that the Pharisees and Sadducees could tell the weather conditions in the physical, but they could not in return tell the spiritual season that they were currently in. Jesus puts emphasis on knowing the spiritual seasons of your life. If you do not know your season, you are like a fish out of water. You are doing a lot of flopping but getting nowhere. Same thing with not knowing your season, you can be expending a lot of energy and gaining nothing. The Pharisees and Sadducees prided themselves on keeping and upholding religious man made laws. They put more importance on their laws and traditions than they did serving God. Their traditions made the power of God to no effect. The two religious groups had become so callused, that they could not realize that they were in the biggest harvest season of their lives. Jesus had come to fulfill the law. Jesus came to set people free.

Jesus came to earth in order to bring the riches of Heaven to earthly vessels. The religious leaders were missing the season. They were so determined to keep their reputation flawless among people that they missed the opportunity to harvest everything Jesus said and did. Get this. You remember all those scriptures that the Pharisees would constantly read to prove themselves to men? Well in those same scriptures, it spoke of a season when God would save humanity from sin once and for all. People from all generations read about that season. Up until that point, that season had lain dormant for centuries. Abraham longed for that season. David constantly wrote and sung about the season that God would save his soul. All the Old Testament saints would have given anything to see that season up close instead of from the distance. Here the Pharisees are standing face to face with the one they have read about their whole lives. The worst part about it is that they do not recognize him. They could not recognize the season they were in. The religious people had an open book test. The answers were found in the scriptures that they constantly read, but still they missed the season. 1 Corinthians 2:8 says if the rulers of this age would have recognized what season they were in, they would not have crucified Jesus. Jesus walked the earth and for the first time people could see the prophesied Messiah face to face. The religious group did not realize that the man who would eventual go on healing the sick, raising the dead, and capturing the hearts of the broken had come to be the first fruits. Sometimes Christians do not realize what season they are in because their dry season and harvest season look the same. My normal is hearing the voice of God. I wake up, pray and allow God to deposit into my spirit. I need to hear every day what God is saying to me. I pride myself on receiving my daily bread from heaven. This should not be abnormal to Christians because Jesus taught this same principle. In the Lord's Prayer, the same one many of us quote from memory, Jesus instructs his disciples to pray "give us this day our daily bread." I take this verse literally. I ask God every day for fresh manna. Some Christians have become complacent and rely on stale bread. These Christians are living on what God spoke to them nine months ago. It is God's will to give us fresh bread. God wants to speak something to us every day. Some people do not have that daily connection with God. Their normal is never hearing God's voice, so when God quiets himself they never know when He isn't speaking. Some Christians do not know the difference between their harvest and their dry season. If your dry season and your harvest season look the same then you have a problem. I always know when God has brought me to a dry season because he quiets himself. If you never take time and listen for God's voice, you will never know what season you are in. This is the same trap Jesus rebuked the Pharisees for. They could discern the physical times but could not discern their spiritual time. If the Pharisees would have correctly discerned the time they were in, their ministries would have looked similar to John the Baptist's. John the Baptist noticed what season he was in. John the Baptist realized that he was in a season of harvest. Why could the Pharisees and Sadducees not see their season? The answer is because they were wrapped into knowing his word rather than his voice. See Christians who know the Word of God sometimes pride themselves on their knowledge of the word. This however; does not mean that you are a follower of Jesus because you know his word. There have been atheists who knew the word better than some Christians. They manipulate the word and start battles with the word. Jesus however did not say that his sheep will know his word but rather that his sheep will know his voice. I pride myself on hearing the voice of God every day. It should be the normal of every Christian's life. We sometimes rely on a word that God spoke to us months ago. When the truth is God wants to speak something to us every day. There are some Christians who only hear God speak at major conferences. What I mean is this. Christians often go to major events with major speakers. At those events a lot of the times God speaks to a person's heart, and they go to an altar where God does tremendous things in their lives. Christians rely on that one event and never hear God speak until the next major conference. This mindset is known as the promise killer. If you rely on stale manna from God, you will eventually abort your God given promise. If you do not get in the habit of receiving "your daily bread," you will eventual kill your promise. Let me explain. God told Abraham to take his promise child Isaac and offer him as a sacrifice. Abraham gave God no lip nor did he put up a fight. Abraham simply obeyed. God spoke to Abraham. It would be like that major conference with all the well-known preachers, and God speaks to us at the altar. God spoke to Abraham at the altar of this mega conference to sacrifice his promise. For most of us, we would have closed our ears and stopped listening for God right after the conferenced close. We would have waited for the next conference or the next "major" preacher. Abraham eventually gets to the mountain that God shows him, and he is about to drive the knife through his promise, and then God tells him not to harm the boy. If Abraham would have not been accustomed to receiving his daily bread, Abraham would have killed his promise. Abraham was in tune with God, he did not only listen at major conferences. If he would have listened only at big church events and instead did not rely on fresh manna, Abraham would have killed his promise. The church is walking around upset at the world because they are becoming less effective. The world has nothing to do with the churches ineffectiveness. The church is settling for a word God spoke twenty years ago and wanting that word to sustain them for the rest of their ministry life. We fall into the same trap as the Pharisees and Sadducees when we cannot discern what season we are in. The church needs to get to hearing God's voice regularly, so when he quiets himself we can discern the transition of our personal spiritual season. If God is always quite in your life and you never hear God, you will never know when you are in a dry season.

The Pharisees and Sadducees came to Jesus and tested him by asking for a sign from heaven. Jesus replied, when evening comes you say, it will be fair weather, for the sky is red, and in the morning, today it will be stormy, for the sky is red and overcast. You know how to interpret the appearance of the sky, BUT YOU CANNOT INTERPRET THE SIGNS OF THE TIMES. Jesus is saying that you can discern the signs of the weather in natural things, but you are blind in discerning the season in spiritual things. It is the job, duty, and responsibility of the religious Pharisaical spirit that is prevalent in the Church today, to blind us to the discernment of spiritual seasons, hence relegating us only to the natural realm. Why does the religious spirit fight with all its power to keep us in the realm of natural thinking? The answer to that question is this. If we accurately discern the times and seasons of our lives, there is powerful and accurate direction from God that will produce His rest accompanied with all its benefits. Discerning the times produces the right decisions. When we walk by His Spirit and lean not on our own understanding, we have stepped into God's sphere. In this place His power and destiny flow into our lives. Everything we set our hands to prospers, we bear fruit for our labor, no weapon formed against us can prosper, and the plan of God is fulfilled in our lives.

It is important to discern the seasons of our lives. Discerning the seasons allows us to correctly gauge what we should do in that season. We would not visit a baseball stadium in midwinter to see a game, neither would we would we expect a major harvest during a time of planting. If you know the seasons, you know what to do, how to pray, and develop an even keener sense of hearing spiritually. By now it should be clear that a powerful kingdom force on earth exist in discerning the times. How much energy and resources have been wasted by not recognizing the spiritual seasons in our lives. If on the other hand, we recognize the times we are in, it will do great good to pray, God give me the grace to not only get through this season in my life, but also let me learn the great spiritual truths that you desire me to have.

Chapter 7
God of Seasons

"To everything there is a season, a time for every purpose under heaven."
Eccl 3:1

Seasons come and go; they have beginnings and ends. There is the season of winter, a time of hibernation and rest. Then there is springtime, a time of planting and new growth. The wise farmer plants in spring, maintains the elements for growth in summer, harvests at the start of autumn, and allows the trees to rest in winter. Knowing the seasons allow the farmer to work in accordance to the tree's activity. The farmer coordinates his activities by seasons because he knows it will produce the most fruit. Just like the seasons of the year, our faith has seasons. Do you know what season you are in? Jesus used the parable of the fig tree (Mat 24:29-31) to illustrate that we need to be aware of our spiritual surroundings and seasons. One of the greatest tragedies for Christians is they do not recognize the seasons they are in. For example, if a Christian is in a winter season and becomes nervous that there does not seem to be any fruit appearing in their life, they may commit to new ministries in order to force themselves to produce fruit. No matter how hard they try, they won't produce fruit until God produces it in them. What is worse is sometimes they blame God for the lack fruit. I can't tell you how many times I've heard "I did everything right, but God didn't come through." God does not fail. However, we fail to recognize our seasons and work with God. There are four seasons that cycle throughout our year. There is spring time, summer, fall and winter. God is the God of all the seasons. Being that the name of the book is "In the dry seasons" our focus will be the dry season, but in this chapter we will briefly touch on all four seasons in order to give a brief overview of each season.

Springtime is a lovely season. The spring is the time of year were dead things begin to blossom. Everyone loves the springtime. During springtime, look for the leading of God in new activities and ventures into new opportunities. On the personal level, these can be activities like new ways of doing your daily devotions or new relationships with encouraging saints. Regarding ministry, springtime can bring new ministry, more attendees or new ways of serving God. Be careful not to invest too much of yourself in all these new things because, just like a fruit tree, not every blossom will lead to fruit. These temporary blossoms serve to pollinate other blossoms. They are also signs to show us that it is springtime.

The summer is the season where fruit begin to appear. This is another season people love. Summer is a time of spiritual development and fruit bearing. Applied to your personal spiritual development, you might find yourself learning to study scripture better, having deeply significant devotions where you feel God's presence more regularly. Applied to your ministry, you might find God giving you strategic insights, you seem to be more effective in your ministry or you have a new sense of anointing. On the other hand, Satan will attempt to divert you; to cause you to put your energies into non-fruit bearing activities. Some of these activities could be attempts to maintain some of the temporary blossoms that were never intended to bear fruit. Summer is a time of spiritual development and fruit bearing.

The next season is fall. During spiritual autumn, our spiritual growth will be shrinking, but the demands from us increase. It is interesting that the greatest harvest of fruit comes when the tree is heading for a season of rest. It is incorrect to say that a person in spiritual autumn does not have God's anointing; God anointing remains on the saints throughout all the spiritual seasons. On a personal level, during spiritual autumn you may be feeling a need to return to the basics of the faith, or a new commitment to the spiritual disciplines of fasting, praying, solitude, individual worship and devotion; things which in themselves, seem to produce little fruit but are essential for our Christian walk.

Lastly, there is winter. This is the season we will mostly speak about because it is in fact the driest of all the seasons. Spiritual winter is the most uncomfortable time for many Christians, especially in the western church. In our western society, we tend to value people based on how much they produce. During spiritual winter, it is normal to feel like God is not hearing our prayers or speaking to us. We may feel like we are having a "wilderness" experience. Our inclination is to pray harder. We want to do anything but remain; but we must remain in the season of rest. We may feel like our ministry is unfruitful and assume it is dying. But during winter, it is a time of spiritual rest. In winter, reflect on God and God's faithfulness to you. Remember to maintain an attitude of reverence before God. It is God's perfect order that all creation rests periodically. God thinks so highly of rest that on the seventh day of creation, He rested too. When we don't rest, we've made our service an idol above God. When we squirm away from spiritual winter, we squirm away from Godliness. We will deal with this season in particular a little later in the book.

God ordains spiritual seasons to provide the greatest spiritual fruit bearing and the greatest spiritual growth. God's seasonal plan includes periods of growth and periods of rest. Recognizing the season you're in and responding appropriately to that season is the best way to insure continued spiritual growth and a life that bears Godly fruit.

8
Plain Ole Dry

Dry- Adj. Free from moisture or liquid; not wet or moist.

Webster's Dictionary

Now that we have the foundations set in stone, we can finally deal with the dry season and what actually occurs during a dry season. According to Webster's dictionary, dry is an adjective that means without liquid or moisture. If you take water away or any other liquid, we find ourselves dry. As soon as you apply water, even just a little bit there is no more dryness. Water or liquid is the fundamental ingredient to dryness. If you have water, there is no dryness. It's the same relationship that we see in light and darkness. Darkness is only darkness until there is light whether it is little light or a light as great as the sun. A dry season is defined by its low humidity, rivers drying up, and animals beginning to leave the dry place to find another place where there is more water. Dryness, stale, withdrawn, stagnant, mundane, thirsty, or just plain stuck. Has anyone felt this way when following Jesus? All these adjectives describe a phase that everyone who is serving the Lord will go through. In this phase, we feel as if God is not hearing us, and we can't understand why He isn't talking to us. Everyone who has counted the cost and is willing to serve God for the rest of their lives will come to a season where they are dry. In the dry season, it feels as if our spiritual growth is lying dormant and even our desires for God grow stale. It is these arid times that are accompanied by impatience, grief, exhaustion, and pre-occupation. These things try to steal our attention from God. Disconnected, tough, uneventful, illogical, uncomprehendable, trapped, or just plain ole Dry.

Back to my third year in college, I was intrigued by the words the lady spoke. Specifically the word about dry seasons had caught my attention. I had urgency in my heart to go home and find everything that I could about dry seasons. I wanted to finally know what I was feeling and why. When I returned home, the lady's statement rang in my head over and over again. I had opened my Bible for only a few minutes and found several examples of great men of God experiencing dry seasons. I began questioning the ladies statement. If it had not been for her, I would have not went home and conducted an intense Bible study trying to get to the bottom of whether there was or was not a dry season. It was through that Bible study that I found countless upon countless Scriptures confirming dry seasons. I realized that day. I was not the first nor would I be the last to encounter what we call a dry season. Great men of faith scattered throughout the Bible all experienced dry seasons. Dry seasons are not unusual to the Body of Christ, but are something normal and healthy. I learned a tremendous amount about the dry season that night. God brought back life experiences to memory to illustrate what happens to a Christian during their dry spell. After I received all this insight on the dry season, God opened doors for me to minister to people. People would randomly text and call to tell me what they were experiencing. None of them knew that God was speaking to me about the very subject.

Psalm 63:1 finds David feeling the same way many of us feel while going through a dry season. David says, "You, God, are my God, earnestly I seek you; I thirst for you, my whole being longs for you, in a dry and parched land where there is no water." This psalm was written when David was fleeing his son Absalom. David had experienced God's power in almost everything that he set out to do. Whether it was killing the bear and lion, standing up to the giant in his land, or establishing Israel as a strong nation, God moved mightily on David's behalf. David was now King. God had promoted David to a position of authority, and now David finds himself in a dry place where his kingship can't help him. Being pastor over a church does not exempt you from the dry season. Seasons are natural, and they show favoritism to no one. The dry season is a testament of how much God loves you. The dry season is part of the process. The dry season is the transitioning period that God is bringing you through to become the man or woman of God He has called you to be. This is a season that shows the intimacy God has for us. God loves us so much that he won't allow us to stay the same. In the dry season, we are forced to mature and depend on God. God loves us so much that he forces us into tough places. The grape must go through crushing in order to become wine. The olive must go through some tough places in order to become oil. God loves us enough to not leave us alone. He is committed to our development. Here is a thought. Man would like to avoid the dry season for one reason. The reason man would love to skip over the wilderness season is because man by nature likes the path of least resistance. We want the easiest path. This is the reason that when I work out, I bring a partner. I hate sit-ups or any exercise that works out the core muscles. If no one is looking I would take a set or twenty off. Because humans love the path of least resistance, you can see it play out in our society now. Fast food restaurants have boomed in the last fifty or so years. No one wants to clean, cook, peel and do the necessary steps that come with cooking. God on the other hand is completely different. God does not operate by the path of least resistance. God by nature operates by the path of greatest glory. God does whatever to bring Himself the greatest amount of glory. Think about this. Out of all the things God could have done to redeem mankind; He chose to send his son Jesus. It is amazing to think that God would give himself knowing the consequences. I'm reminded of the Scripture of Jesus saying, "No one takes my life rather I lay it down." Why did God choose this route, a route that would ultimately lead to his gruesome death? Couldn't have God stopped Adam and Eve from sinning? Couldn't God have stopped the snake in the garden? The answers to these questions are an unequivocal yes, but He didn't because sending Jesus would give Him the greatest amount of glory. See the devil in the garden thought he was getting one over on God. What the devil doesn't realize is that he is overplaying his hand. While the devil is doing something in time, God is sitting in eternity with a plan in place. The Bible says that Jesus was the lamb slain from the foundation of the world. If God would have stopped the serpent in the garden, all Satan would have to worry about is Adam reproducing smaller Adams. Where the devil messed was that he started messing with Adam. Because he started messing with Adam, he made the down payment on a visit from a God named Yeshua. Now the devil doesn't have to deal with a bunch of little Adams. Now the enemy has to deal with a bunch of little Jesus's that have the same Spirit that raised Him from the dead. God's nature is greatest glory. Humans want the easiest path. We see this dynamic play out in the life of Christ. Jesus is one hundred percent man yet one hundred percent God. In the garden of Gethsemane, we see Jesus' human side rise up and want the path of least resistance. In the garden, Jesus human sides pleas for "this cup to pass from Him." On the other hand, Jesus divinity says this is the path of greatest glory. Jesus conquers his flesh and says "not my will, but your will be done." The dry (winter) season is never easy, but it is God's way of getting the greatest glory out of our lives. The dry season pushes us forward into the strong, mature Christians God has ultimately called us to be.

9
Too Close For Comfort

"...A time to plant and a time to harvest." Ecclesiastes. 3:2

The Christian life is a process. It is filled with ups and downs, Mountains and valleys, teachings and test, and spiritual highs and lows. God orchestrates the different seasons in the physical not because He had nothing better to do with his time, but I believe the physical seasonal changes point toward the spiritual seasons of our lives. Ecclesiastes says there is a time for everything a time to sow and a time to harvest. There is a time for us to get up and work and there is a time that we come home and sleep. It is this time of sleep that I love the most (just a side note). Sometimes our spiritual seasons change unexpectedly, and we feel as if we are on this roller coaster ride called Christianity. It is just seasons. What makes dry seasons tougher is that we cannot comprehend the timing of when God decides to lead us into a dry season, and when he decides we come out. It would be much simpler if God would tell me the amount of time I would experience a dry season. I would just hold on for dear life and count the days away until the dry season disappeared, but God does not operate this way. He does not give us fore warning nor does he give us a day to look forward to when the dry season will be over. One day we hear God's voice so clearly. We can feel his presence so strongly. We can sense him guiding our every step. All of a sudden there is a disconnect. We cry out to God and ask where He has gone, but hear no response. In our minds it doesn't make sense. It would be like putting a period in the middle of the sentence. It just doesn't make sense. This is how we view dry seasons. What adds the extra weight is that the human mind always has to have a logical explanation. When we put faith in God, we have to give up our right to understand. God is God, and He does what he pleases. We just need to make sure that we trust him and know He has the plan mapped out for our best.

    I had a friend who attended church regularly for five or six years. She was a leader in the youth group. She was a mentor to many of the youth girls. She would worship God in the altars and attend every youth trip. On Sunday mornings she would help out in any capacity that she could. I remember the day as if it happened yesterday. She Facebook messaged me to tell me that she could no longer feel God. She did not know it and neither did I at the time, but she had just entered into dry season. This was before I knew anything about a dry season. I witnessed her try with all her might to put a finger on what was causing God's presence to seemingly evaporate from her life. The first thing she blamed was the pastor and worship leaders because she couldn't feel God during worship. She complained that the pastor's message was watered down and "it didn't move me." Let me pause here in the story and tell you that it is not the pastor's job to move you. It is not the worship team's job to play songs that you like as an individual. The worship leader is there to carry the burden of leading baby Christians into the presence of God because they do not know how to enter into worship for themselves. The pastor's job is to get a word from Heaven and share that word with the congregation in order that the congregation take the word and make disciples. Do not get me started on the church hopping Christians who jump from church to church because the pastor doesn't "feed them". When I hear that from someone, it shows me your state spiritually. I do not care if you have been serving Jesus for seventy years if you make the statement the pastor does not feed me; it lets me know you are a baby in Christ. Only babies need someone to feed them, hold them, and wipe their butts. If the pastor is preaching from the Bible, then he is feeding you. Our culture has the whole system backwards. When you go to a concert, you should look for entertainment. You should look for your favorite artist to do something that amazes you. This is not the same at church instead of asking what the church can do for you; you should ask what I can do for the church. The pastor's job is not to entertain. If you want entertainment, go to a rock concert. Church services are not meant to be tailored made to an individual's liking. If you have served Jesus for reasonable amount of time, you should be able to get into the presence of God by yourself. If you played a banjo, I would still be able to experience the presence of God. Now back to the story. After she blamed the pastor and the worship team, she turned to look at her own life. One would think that this would be the first thing that she would do before blaming the church, but it wasn't. She started questioning what sin she committed or what sin she omitted. She started looking for the sin in her life that maybe she didn't realize that she had committed. This is the mindset of a lot of Christians who see God as this angry being who is ready to smite every time we do something wrong. Do not get me wrong, we can grieve the Holy Spirit. Grieving the Holy Spirit and God hiding Himself for a season are two totally different things. When we grieve the Holy Spirit, God is quick to convict us and tell us that we have done something. We sometimes view God as the boyfriend that when we do one thing wrong he is quick to move onto another. God is a loving father; he sticks through all our mistakes and tries to help us fix them if we are willing. The key is if we are willing. God does not turn off the rain without warning us. Unrepentant sin can cause God presence to leave, but God isn't the God that leaves without letting you know why. God is not tip toeing out the backdoor while you are a sleep. God always gives warnings before judgment. God convicts us when we have done wrong. God speaks to us when we grieve him. God's word instructs us how to live. When we disobey those instructions, the Holy Spirit convicts us. If we continue to disobey, God gives us other chances to repent. God sends great men and women of God to confirm what he has been telling us. If you continue to disobey after all of this, then God can and will send you into a spiritual drought. There is a difference between a spiritual drought and a spiritual dry season. A drought is not the same as a desert season. The desert season and dry place are supposed to be dry. God leads you to those places. The spiritual drought occurs when you are supposed to be fruitful, but yet God sends no rain because of disobedience. When the Israelites did not experience any rain for three years in the days of Elijah, they were not in a desert. They were still in Israel. The reason God shut off the rain was because of Israel's idol worshiping and disobedience. God did not, however; dry the clouds up without repeatedly asking the Israelites to turn back to Him. Judgment came on Israel because of repeatedly ignoring God's commands. The difference between a spiritual drought and spiritual desert is God walks you into the desert without cause. The spiritual drought, on the other hand, will be caused by disobedience. During the spiritual drought you will be able to point to unrepentant sin as the cause. The spiritual desert and dry season will be uncaused and suddenly. After the young lady decided that she had not done anything that might have played a hand in God's presence leaving her life, she then came to the conclusion that she wasn't doing enough. She felt if she did more that she would feel God. She started praying twice as much and twice as long as she had ever done in her entire life. She started reading her Bible twice as much and twice as long. After all this, she still could not sense the presence of God. By the time she had done all of these things and couldn't come up with an answer to why she could not feel God, the girl eventually gave up on church and God altogether. Her logical reasoning was if I cannot feel God while in church and while praying, there is no point in serving God. What a tragic end friends. God is the best thing that could happen to anyone. There is no reason that I or anyone should abandon God, because the truth is He would never abandon us. She began to party and has been in and out of church ever sense. Remember in one of the previous chapters, a dry season will always entice you to return to your past. Keep in mind this is how the Israelites acted while Moses was on the mountain. It is tempting to think God has forsaken us and because of that we should turn back to the familiar land we have come from. It is your job to remain faithful and strong. If you put your hand to the plow, do not look back.

10

As God Commanded

The whole Israelite community set out from the Desert of Sin, traveling from place to place as the Lord commanded. They camped at Rephidim, but there was no water for the people to drink. ² So they quarreled with Moses and said, "Give us water to drink. "Moses replied, "Why do you quarrel with me? Why do you put the Lord to the test? But the people were thirsty for water there, and they grumbled against Moses. They said, "Why did you bring us up out of Egypt to make us and our children and livestock die of thirst?"⁴ Then Moses cried out to the Lord, "What am I to do with these people? They are almost ready to stone me." Exodus 16:1-5

We all know that God wants to be with us. That was made evident when Jesus took on human flesh and came to earth to dwell amongst us. We do not have a problem with understanding that God wants us to be close to him. The Holy Spirit which is represented by a dove in the scriptures is seen after the flood of Noah. The Holy Spirit flies throughout history landing on individuals for periods of time in order to anoint them for great exploits for God. We see the Holy Spirit anointing Samson, Samuel, and David. All these men where great men, but the dove only landed on them. The next time we see the dove, we see him not only landing but resting on Jesus. The Holy Spirit rested on Jesus while he was here on the earth. Jesus made the statement that it was better for him to go because then the Holy Spirit could indwell believers. Jesus took on human flesh and could only be one place at one time. With his returning to Heaven the Holy Spirit would get his chance to indwell the souls of men. At no other time in history had men had the same opportunity. When Jesus died and the veil was rend from top to bottom, God called his children into a closer relationship. We as Christians have no problem with this thinking. This is why it is hard for us to understand why we enter into a dry seasons. If God wants to be close with us, why does he feel so far away during our dry seasons? The reason the young lady tried to find every reason under the sun to explain why she wasn't experiencing God was because she didn't believe God would voluntarily hide himself from her.

In the scripture at the beginning of this chapter, we read about the Israelites leaving the desert of Sin. The Bible says that they went to wherever God commanded them. God told them the exact places to go. God told them to go to the Desert of Sin. Soon thereafter, they find themselves at a place that has no water. Wait a minute, if God commanded them to go from place to place, and they find themselves at a place that has no water doesn't that mean God commanded them to go to a place that was dry. Earlier in the book we discussed what makes a dry place dry, and it is very complex teaching. Put your thinking caps on for this one. What makes a place dry is that there is no water in that place. Wow what a revelation! Just as no light means darkness. I know very difficult concept to comprehend. The Israelites obeyed God in everything they had done. Their obeying God's direction leads them to a dry place. The first thing to understand about a dry season is that God leads us to them. We do not understand why God would lead us to go to a place that has no water, but is not our jobs to understand just obey.

We can be led by God and still find ourselves in a dry season. We see this with the temptation of Jesus. The Bible says that Jesus being led by the Spirit went into the desert to be tempted. Jesus was led by God to enter into a dry season. God leads us into dry seasons. The story of Elijah being fed by ravens is an incredible story of God's provision. If you are in need to see God's providing hand get in your prayer closet and do what He says. At the end of every obedient Christian is God's supernatural provision. Along with the reminder that God still cares for His children supernaturally, this story also teaches us that God will lead us to dry places. In 1 Kings 17:3-7 tells the story of when God spoke to Elijah and cared for him. Elijah was in Israel while the nation was in a severe drought. God gives Elijah instructions on where to go and what to do. God tells Elijah to go down to a brook. Elijah obeys God goes down to the brook where ravens feed him, and he drinks from the brook. I wish I could end the story here, but the Bible continues this story. The Bible says that the brook eventually dries up. Wait a minute! God told Elijah to go to that brook. God knew that the brook would dry up. Can this mean that God led Elijah to a place that would eventually be dry? Why would God do this? I believe God was teaching us, as well as Elijah that the brook is not Elijah's source. God wanted Elijah to know that as long as he continued to obey his every word, the brook drying up would be yesterday's news because God could provide whatever he needed. God did not want Elijah to become dependent on the brook, The brook was a tool that God used to feed and care for Elijah. God is ultimately the source. We need to keep this in mind when it comes to our jobs. We should not depend on our jobs as the source. Your job is not the source. It may be what God is using for the time, but God is ultimately your source. You can lose your job, but that won't stop God from sending ravens to feed you. We should not rely on our job, but rely on every preceding word that comes from our Father. A dry season is not something that is a result of our transgression against God. A dry season is all God. This should give us more peace in the way we deal with dry seasons. If we recognize that God is the reason for our dry season, then we can trust him that He knows best. If we take the focus off of ourselves and what we did or did not do enough of, we take extra pressure off of our restless minds.

Hide and Peek

We have all had our encounters of experimenting when we were toddlers. I believe it is the toddler stages that we learn the most. We learn the language that is spoken at home. We learn what different objects are and their different uses. Sometimes those curiosities get us into trouble during our youthful years. My toddler days were no different. When I was younger, I was obsessed with the stove. Guess it is just a man's genetics. Men always want to know what is on the stove. We love food. In my toddler days, I was obsessed with the stove. My mom would put a pot on the stove, and I always wanted to touch the pot. The first time I ever tried to touch the pot on the stove; my mom ran to my rescue and told me not to touch the pot because it was hot. At the time, I did not comprehend what hot was. I had not come across anything that was hot. The hottest thing that I had come across was my bath water which was warm. I could not understand why my mom was so bent against me touching a pot that was the same temperature as my bath water. I did not see what the big deal was. Because I did not comprehend the problem, I tried to touch the pot on the stove again. This time my mom took my hand and spanked it. This taught me a lesson. The lesson was not the lesson my mom intended for me to learn however. The lesson my mom wanted me to learn was not to touch the pot on the stove. On the other hand, the lesson I learned was to not touch a pot on the stove, while mom was in the kitchen. I believe a few months passed, and my mind was still curious as to what a pot on the stove felt like. Those few months passed, and I cautiously looked for my opportunity, but mom always stood near the stove. Until one day my opportunity presented itself. I remember my mom putting a pot on the stove, and her leaving me in the kitchen while she went into her room. I saw my chance this was the perfect opportunity to test my theory. I remember tip toeing over to the stove and using my index finger to touch the pot. While my fingers were half way to the pot, I remember seeing out the corners of my eyes my mom coming from her room. I, being the stubborn person that I am could not retract from the mission at hand (literally) because I wouldn't know when the next opportunity would present itself. I see my mom and now my mom sees me. I now know my mom sees me about to touch the pot. As I was mentally preparing for my spanking, my mom did something unusual she did not run to my rescue, she hid behind the wall and did not say a word. She stayed there until I left my finger on the hot pot for an extended period of time and suddenly began to cry. I realized what hot really felt like. It wasn't until this time that my mom stepped from behind the wall and comforted me and told me this was the reason she warned me not to touch the pot. It was the sweetest I told you so I had ever received. I learned never again to touch a hot pot on the stove.

In the dry season it is kind of the same. God sometimes hides himself just to see if we will do what he told us to do when he was talking to us. This is the reason that we should receive daily bread because God will want us to use what He has spoken. Dry seasons to us don't feel very eventful, but they on the contrary are very eventful. Though they feel like nothing is being accomplished, it is just the opposite much is being accomplished. Dry seasons are the seasons of our lives that we learn and grow the most. If my mom would have not remained silent and hidden, I would have still been curious about what hot feels like. If my mom would not have remained silence, I would have never learned not to touch a pot on the stove. Dry seasons are the seasons in which the fire refines the gold. Dry seasons are the seasons that mature us. Dry seasons wean us off of the breast milk and catapult us into mature adult Christians. If we always have breast milk then that is all we would crave. If we live off of breast milk as adults, we become malnourished and unhealthy. The dry seasons are the season where we put to practice what God has been teaching us in the harvest season. The dry season is the test. In any classroom, the teacher gives instructions, tools, and tips. That is until the test is given. The teacher is always quite during the test. The dry season is the test in which God wants to see if he can promote us to the next level. The dry season determines whether God can trust us with deeper truths of his word. One thing about a test and a season is they are temporary. A dry season is still only a season. We sometimes treat it as so much more. Just as day changes to night, and night changes to become day, a dry season will come to an end, and one day it will be done.

A Desert but Not Deserted

It is well known that deserts are dry places. The scorching sun and the minimum amount of water in the desert causes hundreds of deaths each year. Usually the only animals found in the desert are creatures that have scaly skin. Lizards are often found in the desert because they are cold blooded reptiles, and their scaly skin can handle the extreme conditions. The desert has extremely hot days, and the nights are freezing cold. The two extreme temperatures in the desert testify to the roller coaster that we may sometimes feel that we are on in the desert seasons. Just as the lizard, the desert season will try to callus us. We must remember that just because God is hiding himself from our midst, we are in the desert but not deserted. The word deserted comes from the word desert, but God has only temporarily hid himself. You may be in a desert, but you are not deserted. During your dry season, God is still with you. You may not be able to feel him, but God is right by your side. The desert is a tough environment to overcome, but if you overcome the extreme conditions of the desert you can overcome anything. I watch nature channels very periodically. I heard a very interesting comment by one of the guys whose job is to overcome extreme natural conditions. The guy gave an interview about his past experiences and the different ecosystems he has survived. The guy said the hardest environment that he ever tested was the desert. He went on to say after he survived the desert experience, every other ecosystem seemed minor to him. He said he knew after surviving the desert, that he could survive any and every other climate. If you could get through the tough desert environment, there are great things in store for you.

Chapter 11
Always Winter Never Christmas

*"...because I have decided to **winter** there."*

Titus 3:12

I love the winter season, mainly because of my birthday and Christmas. If it would not be for those two things, I would not be a winter fan. I am not fond of cold weather. I am not fond of the stuffy nose I receive thanks to the cold weather. I am not a fan of hot weather either. I guess I am just hard to please. I need the weather just right. Did you know that winter was the driest of the four seasons? The winter season in the physical is the coldest, shortest, and driest. What makes winter different than any other season is that the winter days are short and the nights are long. This makes total sense. Because in our spiritual winter, it seems like we are not being seen by God. It feels as if we are in a spiritual funk. It seems as if our being unseen is one drawn out night. All my life I was taught that plants died during the winter. In elementary school, the teacher would always show a tree empty of leaves to help us understand winter. While this is true that most plants do shed their leaves, it is only half truth. Remember God designed the winter. If we look at what happens in the physical winter, we have clues as to what happens to us in our dry season. This past winter I decided to rake up the leaves in the yard. As I was walked around the yard I saw flowers that were sprouting. You can label me a nerd or geek if you want, but this flower thing caught my attention. I was amazed that a plant was green in the winter. Yes I know I need to get out more. I was intrigued enough by the growth, that I did a little internet study on a process called vernalization. Vernalization (from Latin: vernus, of the spring) is the acquisition of a plant's ability to flower or germinate in the spring by exposure to the prolonged cold of winter." What it basically says is the plant will actually not flower unless it goes through a period of cold. Do you see where I am going with this? I know it often feels like the repeated verse throughout The Lion, the Witch and the Wardrobe, "Always winter, but never Christmas," but truly, without winter, we just may not flower like we are supposed to when it comes time. There are "valleys/winters" and there are "mountains/summers" in life, but I sincerely believe the "valleys/winters" make us who we are. The winters are harsh, but the summer is a whirl of colors and life. Without the winter, we would not appreciate the warmth of the summer. The winter season reignites desperation for God that could be lost. It makes us seek God harder. It makes us thirst after His Spirit more. "Seek while He may be found" Isaiah 55:6. The implication of this verse is that there will come a time or season that you will seek God, and He will not be able to be found. This does not mean that he has left you. It just simply means that He is hiding himself. During those winter seasons, desperation restores inside of us. That desperation sets disciplines and practices that help us when we are going through our springs and summers. My winter seasons have taught me how to seek after God even when God is right by my side. I pray the same way in my spring and summer seasons as I do in my winter. My winters have taught me not to take God's voice for granted. The dry season has shown me what real desperation looks like. When I went through the tough season in my life and it seemed that God had forsaken me, I prayed like I have never prayed before. My heart wanted God so badly. I needed to hear the Father's voice. My heart was so genuine and sincere because I needed God to show himself to me. This carried all the way through into the rest of my seasons. Sometimes especially, during the months where everything is going okay, we can get caught going through the motions. We sometimes pray because that's what Christians are supposed to do. We read our bibles because that's what Christians are supposed to do. We get in a system of checking off our Christianity to do list. This is not the way God intended it. God is not concerned about your Christian to do list. God wants the sincere heart. God wants us to pray to him not so we can say okay got that over with. God wants us to pray, so we can hear his voice. God wants us to worship, so we can enter into his throne room. During those times of harvest, we can be caught praying the "right things." Praying the right things are those prayers we pray nonchalantly because that is what we are "supposed to." God wants us to pray with sincerity. We see this all the time in church. A member of the church asks for prayer for a specific need. The other church members gather around them and pray this nice sweet prayer because that is what Christians are supposed to do. They never pray with compassion or never pray with desperation. The church members pray with their heads and not their hearts. They are not praying to reach the throne room of God. Everything changes when they need prayers for their own lives. You can see a difference in their prayers. The prayers someone prays for someone else and the prayers they pray when they need God to intervene in their own lives are two different prayers. The prayers they pray for other people are nice and cute. The prayers when they are desperate for God are powerful and are not so cute. The nice sweet prayers they pray for the church member look fake compared to the prayers they are praying for themselves in their time of need. The same thing can happen in our spiritual seasons. During those seasons where God is speaking and we feel his presence, we can begin to go through the motions and take the presence of God for granted. Our prayers become sweet and nice instead of desperate and genuine. During those winter seasons, it has taught me to take the same desperation into the harvest seasons of my life. I was convicted when I noticed my prayers looked different depending on what season I was in. I repented to God. I do not want to be desperate for God only when He hides himself from me. Now I pray those ugly, heartfelt prayers whether I am in a dry season or not. I want to thirst for God year round. Americans do not understand the concept of thirsty. If we ever want a drink of water, we can easily turn on the faucet. In Africa where water is not something in abundance, they know the meaning of thirsting.

These people sometimes cry when presented with clean water. I want my life to reflex that I am thirsty for God. This is how I wish to be in my Spiritual life. I do not want to take God for granted. Even in the seasons where I am hearing his voice, my prayers are still going to reflect my desperation for him.

""The Lord our God said to us at Horeb, You have stayed long enough at this mountain." Deut 1:6

The story of God moving the Israelites from Mount Horeb (Sinai) to the Promised Land is another example of God leading us into dry season. The Israelites were pretty content to stay on Mount Horeb. Why wouldn't they? The Israelites saw the smoke. They saw the mountain catch on fire. Though they were a far ways off and were afraid because they heard the thundering in the sky. The Israelites did not get to experience firsthand what Moses did in the mountain. The Israelites were pretty content with staying at Mount Horeb. Moses came off the mountain and his face radiated from the presence of God. If no one else wanted to stay, I'm pretty sure Moses did. To be in a presence so thick that the mountain looks covered with smoke and to be so close to God that you have to hid your eyes because He is walking past. Talk about glory! Moses could have lived on the mountain. Moses could have been content with going up to the mountain for forty days at a time. God had to step in and tell them it is time to move on. See between Egypt (your past life without Christ) and your promise land (the things God has promised you), there is always a wilderness. The wilderness is tough. The wilderness is tough because you know God set you free and led you to this direction, but you do not see any fruit. In your mind's eye you see the promises that God has told you about, but you look around and you see no fruits of that promise. Every once in a while, God will place a mountain in that wilderness. The mountain is just a reminder that God is with you. If you aren't careful you will mistake the mountain for the promise land and want to camp out there. Those mountain top experiences are awesome. I would love for God to walk past me, but the truth is we were not meant to be on the mountain. God purpose is that we walk into the promises that we have for us, but He uses the wilderness to grow us. God said to Moses and his crew in Deuteronomy 1:6, "You have stayed long enough at this mountain." That phrase struck me. How many times has God said, "Sorry, Rontrell' you cannot stay here, you must move on." Sometimes he moves us to a harder place, and sometimes it is to an easier place. Sometimes that place feels like a deep, dark blue canvas of winter, and sometimes it feels like the sandy beaches of the summer. Either way, we need both. When we decide to stay on the mountain or in the valley, we deny ourselves the opportunity to grow because neither is the final destination for us as Christians. The Lord says, you are not at the Promised Land yet, you must keep moving. There is another season and another place I have for you. Where are you? Do you feel the draft of the winter door being left open, or are you experiencing a heat wave of love and excitement? Either way, we will experience both as we are trying to make it to the Promised Land. The final destination is the garden of beauty, and it is always the perfect temperature. Sometimes during our winter months, it feels as if it is always winter and never Christmas.

Come Before Winter

*"...because I have decided to **winter** there." Titus 3:12*

In the bible; winter is not always used as a noun. Paul uses it on multiple occasions as a verb. Paul uses the word in a way that seems particularly strange to our Western culture mind set. If someone says the word winter in America, we think about the season of winter. We think of snow, Christmas, and cold weather. Since I live in Louisiana, I have no idea what the word winter means since we have year round summer. God made a promise that as long as the earth remains there will be summer and winter. The winter referred to in that scripture is the season of winter. There is another way winter can be used. Paul uses it on a few occasions. In the letter that he writes to Titus, he urges Titus his spiritual son to come to him because Paul decided to "winter" at Nicopolis. Paul uses winter as a verb here. When Paul says to winter, he means to wait. Most probably Paul was talking about waiting the winter period out because of the harsh winters that Israel and the relatively close nations experienced. It was hard to travel by sea during the winter because the winds would make the sea dangerous and rough. Traveling in the winter was something that most people would not chance. Like most people, Paul decided to winter in a place that he could stay warm and safe. During the winter, Paul was forced to wait. Paul had to wait for winter to turn into spring. Paul was in his transitioning period waiting on one season to end and another to begin. I believe that this waiting period and wintering period is something that we go through spiritually during our dry seasons. During our driest season which is winter, we are forced to wait. I must admit that I am not one of the most patient people in the world. Because I struggle with my patience, I am smart enough not to pray for it. I understand that God will not wave a magic wand over my head and zap me with patience dust. God will put me in opportunities to practice and learn patience (like driving behind idiots.) I am very goal oriented. God wired me this way. When I have a goal in mind, I cannot rest until that goal is complete. I cannot wait until the next day as long as I have in my mind that something needs to be accomplished. This same mentality sometimes can be overwhelming, especially during my wintering and transitioning periods. I will be transparent and tell you that I am not the biggest fan of waiting periods in my life. The dry season in my life was the toughest thing that I have been through in my Christian walk because it forced me to wait. When there is a task that is branded on my mind, I hate wasting time. I feel like if will be wasted that it should be wasted while I have nothing else to do. I hate wasting time when there is something that needs to be done. I do not like doing things multiple times when it could have been done right the first time. I remember moving furniture for a "LADY", and she was so indecisive. Indecisive and lady in the same sentence go figure (yep to late you are ready brought the book.) We would move the furniture one place, and she wouldn't like the way it looked in that place. She would then want us to move it to another place. In my mind, I was banging my head against the wall. My thoughts were that she should have decided where she wanted her furniture before she had us come over. Being the nice guy that I am, I was stuck three hours moving furniture back and forth. My last dry season made me feel the same way. I felt like there were so many things that I needed to get accomplish, but I was stuck. I can imagine Paul wanting to visit the churches that he planted, but having to wait in his winter period because there was nothing he could do about it. In your dry season you will feel stuck. You will want to move on and skip this season.

You may feel caged in and all alone. While Paul was stuck in Nicopolis, he had to endure his dry season by "wintering." While we may feel stuck the dry season gives us opportunity to tap into our destiny. When we are in our dry season, we may feel like we are at a standstill in our walk with God. I will prove to you otherwise. We may not feel like we are progressing in the dry season, but it is the dry times that catapult us into our God-given destiny.

■■■■■■■

I love watching TV. I mostly watch sports. I am a diehard anything Louisiana sports fan. You may not want to watch a New Orleans Saints game with me. You may question the work God has done in my life. You know that patience I struggle with; well I think God made me a Saints fan because that may be the only way I will pray for it. Other than sports on TV, I like to watch things that I can learn from like the discovery channel. I love watching the discovery channel. I remember watching a show on the discovery channel and the show was about black crows and some of the unusual things that have been captured on camera. In this one instance, a civilian with a camera caught a shot of some crows. The camera then zoomed for a closer shot; I found a larger brown bird sitting on a street lamp. The bird was a young eagle. The crows circled over him and tried to attack him. Whenever they attacked, the eagle's head turned toward them, and he spread the wings and was ready to defend. I wondered what made the crows even have the audacity to attack a young eagle. I also wondered why the eagle did not fly away. Then I noticed that the eagle had a damaged left wing. There was a large hole in his wing and there were missing feathers, which prevented him from flight or fight. Normally a crow dares never to attack an eagle. Even though he was quite young, in this case the bird was injured and therefore helpless. The crows saw an eagle that was stuck and they jumped at the opportunity. It is known that Satan will mostly attack us when we are most vulnerable and unable to fight. Every few years the eagle goes through a phase when they gradually lose their old feathers. In this stage it is initially difficult to fly, and after the loss of the old feathers it becomes completely "grounded." Its only option is to wait to grow new feathers. This is what the dry season does. It forces us to transition from something old into something new. We begin to mature. We are forced to wait until God revels himself to us again. Transition is always frustrating. The enemy attacks us most when he feels we are vulnerable. When we are vulnerable is when Satan begins to throw fiery darts at us tempting us to question God. Questions like why would God leave. Questions saying we are not good enough. Satan even tempts us to compare our situations to other surrounding Christians in order to make us insecure about our own walk with God. We become like the grounded eagle vulnerable and waiting.

■■■■■■■

Winter develops certain characteristics and values, which are unable to produce in your life any other time of the year. It is a time of purification, which God uses in your life to lead to a higher level of spiritual development. The following are features developed in the winter: gentleness, patience, compassion, kindness, love, etc. You are able to show empathy to others, because I know very well how they feel. You'll also be able to better appreciate God's grace and mercy, and realizing our own weaknesses, gain humility and obedience to Him. Winter cleanses your spirit and soul and makes you continue to grow. There are also negative pitfalls of winter also. We can learn how to recognize Satan's schemes, in order to avoid them. As I have previously stated, Satan pounces on the Christian in their dry season. He jumped at the opportunity to tempt Jesus in his wilderness experience. If we keep this in mind, we can be more guarded and aware. Feelings of worthlessness and failure are among the top emotions related to the dry season. Everyone that I come in contact with who is dealing with a dry season tells me that they are doing something wrong. We think this because we think God's presence left us because of something we did. Do not brood over the feelings of worthlessness. This is just the enemy trying to cause you to abort the destiny God has for you. Finding relief in the wrong people is another characteristic. It is easy to find relief in the wrong people during the dry season. It was uncomfortable hanging around my classmates who were experiencing their mountaintop season, because it constantly reminded me of the season I was in. I wanted the mountaintop, but I was dry. I compared my walk with my classmates, and by doing that I felt inferior because God was talking to them and not me. During the winter season, it is easy to miss church because seeing others worship God reminds you about those times you could worship God and sense his presence. It only worsens the situation. If you give into the feeling you become isolated. The enemy likes nothing better than an isolated believer. The Bible tells us to carry each other's burdens. The reason for this is when one brother or sister is weak the family can pick up the slack. The bible says a threefold chord is not easily broken. When you become isolated, you have no one picking up the slack. The enemy is isolating you because you are a weak target. If you do not give into those feelings and continue to fight through, the enemy cannot target you out because you have brothers and sisters carrying your burdens. The main thing to remember is that your refuge is in God! When you're physically and mentally exhausted, it's easier getting you to doubt, fear and worry. Relax, partake of the Lord and cast your cares on Him. Meditate on his promises for your life, and in this way you strengthen your faith. If you do not put the dry season in right perspective, there could be a sense of rejection. It is easy during the dry season to feel as though God is rejecting us. Each one of us to a greater or lesser degree has suffered rejection, but some more than others. When you feel rejected, you tend to be isolated from the environment. During the dry season it is easy to sit in your room and pout. It is easy to isolate away from your friends and loved ones. When you feel rejected, you can also begin to consciously or unconsciously reject others. Do not make any important decisions in this state of soul, because the feelings of abandonment and uneasiness that come along with the dry season can cause you to easily make a mistake or say the wrong words. These are some of the characteristics of a dry season. Remember during the winter seasons of our life, the devil knows we are vulnerable and will try to his hardest to make us stumble. The devil did it to Jesus.

12

The Pain of Waiting

> *⁸ And after the whole nation had been circumcised, they remained where they were in camp until they were healed.⁹ Then the Lord said to Joshua, "Today I have rolled away the reproach of Egypt from you." So the place has been called Gilgal to this day.¹⁰ On the evening of the fourteenth day of the month, while camped at Gilgal on the plains of Jericho, the Israelites celebrated the Passover. ¹¹ The day after the Passover, that very day, they ate some of the produce of the land: unleavened bread and roasted grain. Joshua 5:8-11*

There is strong Revelation that could be gained from the eagle during his waiting period. Throughout my ministry life, there is one thing that hurts more than anything else. It hurts more than backbiting Christians and hurts more than leaders not being on the same page. The thing that I am referring to is transition. Just mentioning the word sends chills up my spine. My last transition was not fun at all. The sitting and waiting was severely frustrating. May I be so bold and say that trusting God was hard. I remember as if it was yesterday, the long stressful nights of waiting for

God to open a door. I prayed that any door would open. Day after day waking up knowing that God called me, knowing that God placed destiny inside me, but seeing with my physical eyes the same thing I saw the day before. This is the same thing Paul faced when he told Titus I have decided to winter here. Paul was forced to wait until the season passed. Paul had to wake up each morning looking forward to making his journey to the different churches, but he had to settle for waiting until his winter season passed. Paul had to wait for his transition from winter to spring. The dry season forces us into transition. Waiting is no fun. The dry season is one long transition and there is pain in waiting.

■■■■■■■

The Israelites faced the same problem. Before I explain what the Israelites faced, let me give some context. The Israelites came back with bad reports from the promise land, so God sent them in circles over the desert for forty years. The Israelites were promised a land flowing with milk and honey. When they get to the land, they were afraid of the giants of the land. God then sent them circling around the desert for forty years until the older generation died. Here is where our story begins. The children of the older generation had traveled in the desert forty years with their parents. I can imagine the older generation telling the younger generation about a land flowing with milk and honey. I can imagine that the older generation telling remarkable accounts about the size of the grapes that the land bore. For forty years, the younger generation dreamed about living in the land. They would walk around the desert dreaming of the day when they no longer had to be temporary residents of the desert, but would inhabit the promise land God had foretold. After forty years, they find themselves near the promise land; and the only thing separating them from the promise land was the Jordan River. Can you imagine their eyes lighting up? Can you see their mouths begin to water when thinking about the massive grapes? Can you see their thoughts about finally stepping into the promise land? The dreams they had at night were soon about to turn into reality. The Bible then tells the account in Joshua 5. The Israelites crossed the Jordan River and are about to enter into the promise land. Before you get to happy and think that is the end of the story, let's look at the passage. The Bible says that Joshua took a flint knife and circumcised the men of Israel. Because of this, the men had to stay in their tents to heal. Could you imagine this? The Israelites were so close. They had waited their whole life to enter the promise land, but they find themselves in pain and waiting to heal. Transition is always painful. Dry seasons hurt. Dry seasons go hand in hand with transition. Israel was going through a period of transition. Their desert period was behind them, but they weren't in the promise land yet. They were stuck in a middle period. They were out of the desert, but not in the promise land either. When we are so close to God's promise, we want to do anything but wait. We become anxious and our excitement is uncontrollable. When we are ready to head into God's promise and are forced through transition, we become unsettled and frustrated. Waiting is painful. The anticipation to get to the promise land was prolonged even more. Why does transition always hurt? Why are the dry seasons so uncomfortable? The answer is because God is cutting away on our flesh. Why is the dry season so frustrating? It is frustrating because there is nothing you can do about it. When you cannot control the outcome of a situation, you are forced to trust God. I am very stubborn. I want things done my way. When I do not have a say in the matter, it is very uncomfortable. The men of Israel were in a very uncomfortable position. I can laugh at their situation because they were extremely uncomfortable. Talk about hurting. OUCH! God before he allowed them to enter into the promise land cut away flesh. When God begins to remove our flesh and its desires, it hurts. God cannot allow you to enter your promise land with fleshly desires. When we take up our cross, we are killing our flesh. Death is never easy. When we kill our flesh it hurts. If we never kill our flesh, we become susceptible to moral failures. I have read and heard about countless pastors who failed morally. Whether it was with finances or sexually, I find there is one thing with most cases. The one thing I find is they did not allow God to cut away their flesh. Those pastors admittedly rushed into the promise land. On one occasion one of those many pastors told the story of his failure. He began by saying his moral failure did not start when he pocketed the churches money. The pastor said his failure started when he rushed into his promise land. He told the story of him being in a transition phase, and he felt God doing an incredible work on him. The pastor said he knew God was about to open a position in ministry, but he rushed into it. Right in the middle when God was cutting away flesh and allowing him to heal, the pastor interrupted the process and rushed into his promise land. The dry season is a time of transition. The dry season is the time God removes and cuts away flesh. To deny the dry season is to deny your destiny. The pastor failed morally because in his transition, he did not allow God to cut away his flesh. The gifts of God open doors for you, but it is character that keeps you there. Character is built in the dry season. The Bible then says the Israelite men were stuck in their tents until they could heal. The reason the Israelites had to wait was because they had to heal. If Joshua would have never circumcised the Israelites, they would have no reason to heal. If they had no reason to heal, they would have no reason to wait. Our waiting periods and times of transition have everything to do with us healing. During our dry seasons, it is a time of healing. God cuts away our flesh because he cannot allow us to enter into the promise land with certain things. Joshua circumcised them and it hurt. Transition and winter periods always make us feel stuck, and they always hurt because our flesh is being cut on. It is easy to serve God when everything feels okay, but it hurts to pray to a God you feel isn't listening. It hurts to go to church and witness worship moving other people but not you. Winter seasons hurt. God told Joshua after he had circumcised the men that now the sins of Egypt had been rolled away. If it had not been for the pain of the transition and winter, the reproach of Egypt would not have been rolled away. God cut away their past. God could not allow them to enter into the promise land with their past still connected to them. The circumcision was a sign that there past was removed. The transition period is the result of healing taking place. Though the winter waiting period is where you feel stuck and uneventful, it is full of activity. Instead of taking possession of the promise land, the Israelites were stuck in their tents.

Joshua chapter five says that it was on the tenth day that the Israelites got circumcised and did not heal until the fourteenth day. How do you overcome your winter and transition period? The Bible tells us in Exodus 12:3-6.

> *³ Tell the whole community of Israel that on the tenth day of this month each man is to take a lamb[a] for his family, one for each household. ⁴ If any household is too small for a whole lamb, they must share one with their nearest neighbor, having taken into account the number of people there are. You are to determine the amount of lamb needed in accordance with what each person will eat. ⁵ The animals you choose must be year-old males without defect, and you may take them from the sheep or the goats. ⁶ Take care of them until the fourteenth day of the month, when all the members of the community of Israel must slaughter them at twilight.*

On the tenth day of the month, it just so happened that Joshua circumcised the Israelites. This is the same day according to Exodus 12:3-6 that a household was to bring a lamb into the house and take care of it in preparation for Passover. The Israelites did not heal until the fourteenth day. It just so happens that the fourteenth day is the day they are to sacrifice the lamb. From the tenth day to the fourteenth day the Israelites were stuck in their tents waiting to heal. It was also on the tenth day that the households of Israel would bring in a lamb and take care of it. From the tenth day of the month to the fourteenth day of the month, the Israelites were in pain and waiting. It was these days that the lamb was found in their tents. The only way to deal with your winter and transition season is to get intimate with the Lamb. The Israelites had no choice they were stuck. When we feel stuck what more can we do but get intimate with the Lamb of God, Jesus. What seems to be hopeless, it may be full of promises for the future. Note that the waiting time is not wasted period. You learn patience and perseverance. It is also the time to bury the old and birth something new. It is the time of renewal. Take the example of the Apostle Paul. At the end of his service, he experienced many restrictions in jail; he was like the "grounded" eagle. In spite of his adversity and in spite of him being stuck, he birth most of what we call the New Testament. In this very difficult time, he formed the letters of Paul, which still serve all believers. Because Paul was grounded and forced to wait in jail and Nicopolis, it catapulted him into his destiny. Part of the plan God had for Paul was for Paul to write 2/3 of the New Testament. If Paul wasn't forced into a waiting seasons, he would probably not have written what we call today the Bible. "In the shadow of his hand he hid me, make me an arrow in a smooth, in his quiver I hid" (Isaiah 49.2). Sometimes God hides his warriors in a waiting period. He does this in order that we become an arrow in the quiver. These are no ordinary shots. They have a special purpose and are prepared for a specially chosen moment. When it comes, it will be released out of the closet (Ps 18.15). God in his wisdom knows that sometimes it is better not to expose his servants to the shelling of the enemy. Premature entry into the service can be disastrous. If a man has not been properly prepared, he is not sufficiently mature. Can you imagine the Israelites taking control of the promise land with their past still attached to them? Instead of enjoying the blessings of serving God, they fall in an ambush. Joseph embraced his waiting and dry season. A long stay in prison until it was time for his exaltation in Egypt caused Joseph to be the man of God he was! Moses lived in the desert 40 years before God called him back to Egypt, and he eventually led his people from bondage. If the Israelites would have entered the promise land without the reproach of Egypt being taken away, the Israelites would have only reproduced Egypt in the promise land. God, however; forced them into a waiting period by cutting away fleshly desires.

    The apostle John found himself isolated on an island called Patmos. John was isolated on the island because of his testimony about Jesus Christ. It is here on this certain island that John was trusted with the Revelation of Jesus Christ. Patmos was known as a sterile island according to most scholars. The island being sterile simply means unable to produce. The Romans would cast criminals on this island to die. The word Patmos could be translated "my killing." In this dry, sterile place that had the potential to kill was the very place God wanted to bring John this tremendous revelation of Jesus. This thought made me wonder. In the book named after him, John refers to himself as the disciple that Jesus loves. This same John was the disciple that rested his head on Jesus' breast at the Last Supper. John relationship with Jesus ran deep. John was one of the only disciples that could be found at Jesus' crucifixion. To solidify Jesus' and John's relationship further Jesus while He was on the cross entrusted his mother to John. No doubt Jesus trusted John. Without question John was found faithful. Why could God not give John this glorious revelation at another point in John's ministry? God decided to use this particular place in John's life to show him this deep revelation. I am convinced that God uses our Patmos's of life to produce the greatest revelation of who Jesus really is to us. Patmos was John's dry season. No doubt John felt stuck. I do not question whether or not John felt as if God abandoned him. John never took the position on whether he was being treated fairly or not. John kept his heart right in order to receive from God even in the most sterile place of his life. Foundation on which a building stands is not visible, and the higher and larger buildings, have a deeper and more solid foundation. Therefore, it is important that the foundation of your life be firm, before God will extend the length and breadth.

13

Dry Season = Destiny

God has showed me some tremendous insight on the spiritual aspect of dry seasons. None of that insight gets deeper than the things found in this chapter of the book. I was under the impression that since my dry season felt so bland that there was nothing happening physically or spiritually. I could not have been any more mistaken. I have hinted all throughout the book that Satan attacks in no other season more than in the dry season. First before we get into the meat of the chapter let me lay a foundation. Satan is our enemy. We are Satan's enemy. The Bible says that we wrestle not against flesh and blood, but against rulers and principalities. A Christian's life involves and is surrounded by constant warfare. It is in the Christian's job description to be in a fight. Some Christians do not have to fight the devil because they are not a blimp on the devils radar. The devil isn't afraid of them because they are doing nothing to advance the kingdom of light. Jesus says if you are not for me you are against me, and he who does not gathers with me scatters. Here is a revelation. If you are doing nothing, then you working against Christ. Christians must understand that our fight is not against flesh and blood but against Satan and his kingdom. The best news about it all is that we have already won. We are in a fight that is already won. Greater news is that we do not have to fight with our own power. Jesus has given us his Spirit, power, and authority. We can super impose the kingdom of light over the kingdom of darkness.

We have briefly discussed that our dry season is a test from God. The reason that God seldom speaks during a dry seasons is because a teacher never speaks when giving a test. What does a test accomplish? It either graduates or hinders a student from advancing to the next level. During those times when God is speaking to us on a regular basis, he is teaching us. When the time comes when he shuts himself up, the test has begun. At this point God wants to see whether we can use what he has given us.

When it comes to teaching arithmetic to little first grade girls, let me put it out there, it is not my calling. I have a godchild that was learning how to do addition. This is where my lack of patience kicks in. I was attempting to help her with her addition problems. I would stand over her and instruct her. When I was standing over her, she would get every one right. It could have had something to do with me practically telling her the answers, do not blame me blame my patience. I saw that I was being too much of a help to her and that she was not really learning anything, so I decided to step back and let her do a couple on her own. When I returned to check her work, she had not gotten any right. I realized that she had only gotten the others right because I was instructing her how to get the right answers. As long as I would stand over her shoulder and not allow her to put into practice what I at least tried to teach her, she would always rely on me standing there and her growth would be stunted. God is the same way. If God would always give us the right answer while standing over our shoulder, we would always rely on God to give us the right answer. We would never grow and our spiritual growth would be stunted. We would only know the right things to do because the answer was given to us on a silver platter. The test is when the teacher is silent, and the test proves what we really learned. The devil would like nothing better than to hold up our progress in God. It is during the dry season that we wrestle with the enemy the most. It is the devil's goal to influence us to fail our test. Our destiny is inherently connected to our dry season. If we allow the enemy to influence us in our dry season, we allow him to influence our growth. Later in the chapter, I will prove this to you.

    I believe that dry seasons are a test from God. They mature us and develop us into stronger Christians. I believe that dry seasons are the part of our life that we are to incorporate what God has been teaching us and what we have learned. Dry seasons are extremely important to us as Christians. Christians are sometimes Christians only because everything is going swell. Christians can begin to idolize the stage in life where everything is okay. I have been guilty of doing this. Christians look back to a time when they felt they were at their pinnacle. Christians look back and reach for the time in their life when they were on fire. I have been guilty of doing the same thing. I remember praying one day "God rekindle the fire that I had back in such and such." God quickly rebuked me and told me that I was putting him in a box. He asked why I would look back to the "glory days" when he promised to take me from "glory to glory."

He said that the fire that I experienced in the past was little compared to the fire he has in store for me. He told me as long as I prayed looking back; I would cripple what He could do in my life. God wanted to ignite a fire ten times of what I had before. As long as I prayed for the old glory, God could only give what I prayed. Simply put I was putting a ceiling on my prayers. It is similar to the story of Elisha the prophet and King Joash found in 2Kings 13. King Joash came to Elisha seeking counsel on defeating the Syrian army. Elisha tells King Joash to take out an arrow and shoot it out of the window. King Joash does as the man of God commanded. Elisha then tells King Joash to take another arrow out of the quiver and beat it on the ground. King Joash takes out an arrow and beats it three times. Elisha, the man of God, becomes angry with Joash. Elisha tells him he should have beaten the arrow six or seven times because then Israel would strike Syria until they were defeated. Because the king only struck the arrow three times, he would only strike Syria three times. Since the king limited his strikes, God was limited in what He could do. If we pray for the three strike prayer instead of the six or seven, you get the results of the three strikes. When we pray, God rekindle the fire that I had once upon a time, you are limiting God. It is as if you are striking the ground three times. Here is another nugget. If you pray God I want Pentecost as the apostles had, you are limiting God. God is a God who saves the best for last. The Bible says the latter rain will be greater than the former. We are supposed to go from glory to glory. Pentecost was not God's greatest performance. God saves his best for last. What happened on Pentecost was just the beginning of what God wants to do. If we pray, God we want Pentecost as the disciples had, we are limiting the glory that God wants to bring to us today. After God showed me this, I began to quickly pray God I want all "your fire." We sometimes get to a place where we are reaching for a time instead of reaching for God. We get caught in comparing seasons. When we look at this closely, comparing seasons does not make much sense. How idiotic would a farmer in the winter say, "Man last spring I produced more fruit than I am right now in the winter." I would look at the farmer cross eyed. It makes sense that you aren't producing more fruit in the winter than the spring because in the spring is the time when things begin to blossom. If we think about it in that context, why do we say the same thing as the farmer? In our winters, we often look at our springs and want what we had in the spring. Every Christian wants the mountain top experience that Moses encountered. I have never heard anyone say to me I want the valley experience. Did you know that the water flows from the mountain into the valley? The snow at the top of the mountain melts and flows to the valley. The green plants grow in the valley. The valley is where one has the ingredients to grow. The valley is important, yet no one sees the importance of going through the valley experience. Christians find themselves only being able to praise God during the spring and summer seasons, those are the seasons that take the less sacrifice in terms of our spirit man. Christians only want to praise God when the sacrifice isn't a huge cost. We must find ourselves in the same faith that David found himself when he said "I will not offer to God nothing that cost me nothing." Real sacrifice cost something. If you are only praising God when everything is okay, then it really isn't praise at all. Praise is a sacrifice and sacrifice always cost something.

Homeless

"When an impure spirit comes out of a person, it goes through arid places seeking rest and does not find it. Matthew 12:43

Dry seasons challenge our faith and trust in God. Jesus told Thomas after He resurrected, "Blessed are those who have not seen and yet believe." There is a special blessing and special anointing that comes among believers when we can't see God or feel Him, but I still believe. I believe God pours another anointing over our lives when we do not see God, but yet still believe him. we have to truly believe God when God is not looking over our shoulder and telling us the answers. True belief starts when you unhesitantly do what God ask. When we can't see God and when God hides himself is when your level of faith and trust is revealed. Jesus spent 33 years on earth. Three of those years were filled with hands on training of the disciples that would eventually go on to start the church. Everywhere Jesus went the disciples were right with Him. They saw Him every day. They talked, ate, and slept with him until his death. After Jesus' resurrection, He appeared to the disciples over a span of forty days. He would appear to the disciples and then disappear. He would walk through locked doors and then suddenly leave. I personally believe Jesus was teaching them that He will be as present with them in the invisible as he was in the visible. I believe he was teaching us that we can trust Him even when we can trace Him. Even in those seasons of our lives where we can't take our finger and trace where God is, we can still be confident that we can trust him. There will be times in our lives where God will be hard to trace, but even when He seems invisible we can trust Him. Dry seasons are important because there is an anointing that comes upon your life when you prevail even though you do not see God. What about the opposite is there consequences if we fail a dry season? I said a test can graduate or hinder us. Can how we respond to our dry season hinder us as well? First I want to say that God is rich in his mercy, grace, and forgiveness; but there is a place where you can fail your test. When we don't implement what God has taught us in the dry season, we fail our test. Most people do not realize the importance and significance of dry seasons. They underestimate the value of the dry season. They think because they are spiritually drained and dry that there is no spiritual activity going on. This could not be further from the truth. There is an important spiritual molding that goes on in the desert. If our destiny is connected with our dry season, don't you think the devil would try his best to keep us from fulfilling our God given destiny. There is a lot of spiritual activity that goes on when you are in your dry place.

■■■■■■■

Jesus gives us a spiritual glimpse of the spirit realm when he says, "When an impure spirit comes out of a person it goes through arid places seeking rest and does not find it." Jesus gives the description of what happens to an evil spirit once it is cast out of a person. It is interesting what Jesus says. Jesus says that the spirit goes to arid places. Arid means dry. It means waterless in the Greek. Jesus was talking in the physical, but also the spiritual because demons are spirits. Demons, once they are evicted from a person and become homeless, travel to dry desert places in order to seek rest. There is a lot of spiritual activity while you are in your dry season because your dry season is connected to your destiny. Satan would like more than anything than to keep you from your spiritual designation in God. The good news is if you're a Christian the demon cannot find rest in you because your temple has been bought. Greater is He that is in you than he that is in the world. Though the enemy cannot abide in you, that will not stop them from trying to influence you. It is our dry seasons that we are the most vulnerable and we are more easily influenced. Every Christian in an arid place is surrounded by the enemy. The devil wants to distract us and get us off course. If he tried to entice Jesus in His dry season, how much more should we be on guard? Keep in mind should you will be determined to past the test. Though you can't feel Him, God is still there. It is our dry seasons that the enemy influence is the most prevalent. They are seeking rest in the dry places. When we are dry, we face the most spiritual warfare in our lives. In researching for this book, I interviewed countless of Christians who proclaimed they were experiencing a dry season. The number one thing they all had in common was they were always tired and drained. Physically they had trouble waking up and trouble going to sleep. Why is this? I preach every Wednesday night in our student ministry. No other night during the week am I so drained? The reason is because our spirits are warring with the kingdom of darkness. The reason tiredness is commonly accompanied with the dry season is because your spirit is fighting. We must realize that we do not fight against flesh and blood. The devil has a strategy. Our dry seasons play an important role in our destiny. This is the reason demons search the dry places. They would like nothing better than to keep us away from our destiny.

Can I prove my point further? Jesus before he started his ministry went to the desert. The desert is a dry and arid place. When Jesus was in the desert, the devil tempted him. Now the Bible says that Jesus was tempted in all ways but yet without sin. Well in the temptation of Jesus that is recorded in scripture, Jesus was not tempted in every way. The Bible only records three different temptations. Three different temptations does not equal tempted in every way. After the temptation in the desert, the Bible does not record Jesus being tempted ever again. Why weren't all the other temptation accounts recorded. Why was this specific instance of temptation the only recorded? The answer is easy this temptation of Jesus was the most important. Jesus was one hundred percent man as well as one hundred percent God and was tempted throughout his life on earth. If the Bible wrote about every temptation of Jesus it would be extremely long, but God took time to note this specific time Jesus was tempted. None of the others were more important than this temptation. Jesus had just been baptized. He was about to start the road to his destiny, and the Holy Spirit led him to the desert. Our destiny is always connected to our desert seasons. Before Jesus could step into his destiny, he had to step into his desert season. While he was in his desert season, the devil comes. Our arid places will always have enemy activity. While we feel the desert season is uneventful, the spiritual activity is non-stopped. There is continuous warfare going on around you during your dry season. The devil tempted Jesus in his desert season because he knew the importance of what Jesus had to accomplish. If the devil could get Jesus to fail while he was weak, then he would not have to worry about Jesus anymore. Be alert while you are in your dry season. Do not be surprise if old girlfriends call and want to hang out. Do not be surprised if that group of friends you haven't spoken to in years decides they want you to come over. Remember we are not wrestling against flesh and blood. Our dry season make us weary and drains our spirit man. The devil realizes this and would like nothing better to get you to fail. Our destiny in God destroys the devil's foothold in the world. Do not give way to the enemy during your dry season. The deeper you walk with God the more intense your testing will be. Stay grounded and rely on what God has taught you. Soon your angels will come and minister to you.

Don't Do It

20 In the first month the whole Israelite community arrived at the Desert of Zin, and they stayed at Kadesh. There Miriam died and was buried. [2] Now there was no water for the community, and the people gathered in opposition to Moses and Aaron. [3] They quarreled with Moses and said, "If only we had died when our brothers fell dead before the Lord! [4] Why did you bring the Lord's community into this wilderness, that we and our livestock should die here? [5] Why did you bring us up out of Egypt to this terrible place? It has no grain or figs, grapevines or pomegranates. And there is no water to drink!" [6] Moses and Aaron went from the assembly to the entrance to the tent of meeting and fell facedown, and the glory of the Lord appeared to them. [7] The Lord said to Moses, [8] "Take the staff, and you and your brother Aaron gather the assembly together. Speak to that rock before their eyes and it will pour out its water. You will bring water out of the rock for the community so they and their livestock can drink." [9] So Moses took the staff from the Lord's presence, just as he commanded him. [10] He and Aaron gathered the assembly together in front of the rock and Moses said to them, "Listen, you rebels, must we bring you water out of this rock?" [11] Then Moses raised his arm and struck the rock twice with his staff. Water gushed out, and the community and their livestock drank. [12] But the Lord said to Moses and Aaron, "Because you did not trust in me enough to honor me as holy in the sight of the Israelites, you will not bring this community into the land I give them." Num. 20:1-13

Just as we can pass our test, we can also fail a dry season. The dry season is our test. It shows how much we trust God in the hardest spiritual battle in our lives. God speaks to us and then quiets himself so that we can take the test. How we use what God has taught us in the dry season, can determine if we get promoted or not. Can our destiny be affected for the worst in a dry season? The answer to that question is yes. A student who consistently fails an algebra test must retake the course. A year of his life must be spent redoing what they should have learned the first time.

Deuteronomy 1:2 says, "It takes eleven days to go from Horeb to Kadesh Barnea by the Mount Seir Road." Horeb is better known as Mount Sinai. Mount Sinai is the place where Moses had his mountain top experience. From Mount Sinai to the promise land usually took one family eleven days. Granted that the Israelites had approximately two million to three million people traveling during their exodus from Egypt, their trip should have taken up to forty days depending on how fast they traveled. Their desert experience took forty years. You can extend your duration in the desert if you do not embrace it. The Israelites grumbled, complained, and looked at everything that was negative. Their forty day journey turned into a forty year journey. If we do not embrace our desert season, we can extend how long we are in the desert. We should look at our desert season as God transforming us from glory to glory. God is maturing us. The desert is only a place that will benefit us in the long run. Do not focus on the here and now because if you do, you will end up like the Israelites who wanted to go back into Pharaoh's captivity. They couldn't understand why

God had brought them out into the desert to die. They didn't realize that they had to go through the desert to get to the promise land. Everyone wants the resurrection glory, but no one wants the death and pain that comes before resurrecting. Everyone wants to see miracles, but no one wants the consecration and dedication that comes with having a miracle filled life. Everyone wants the shine of gold but no one is willing to go through the fire and be refined. The desert seasons only mature us. If you are going through a desert, keep on plowing because your promise land is coming soon.

How we perform in the desert can also affect our destiny altogether. We can use Moses as an example. The Bible says that the Israelites and Moses arrived in the Desert of Zin and there was no water. Moses was in the desert, but not only was Moses in a dry place, but he had to lead people while he himself was in a dry place. There is nothing like pastoring an ungrateful people while you are going through a desert place. Moses goes before God, and God tells him what to do about the ungrateful people. God tells Moses to speak to the rock. In his dry season, Moses doesn't do what God tells him to do. Moses strikes the rock twice when God told him to speak to the rock. Moses disobeys God out of frustration.

Because Moses disobeyed God in his dry season, Moses alters his destiny and God did not allow Moses to enter into the promise land. Moses' disobedience in his dry season caused his future in the promise land to be cancelled. Moses did not heed what God spoke to him. God speaks to us and then quiets himself wanting us to put into practice what He has said. Don't you think that God could have sent an angel to stop Moses from hitting the rock? God did send an angel to stop Abraham from sacrificing Isaac. God could have, but the point was this was Moses test would he listen or disobey? God wanted to see if Moses would put into practice what He spoke to him. Our dry seasons are extremely important. Moses was the pastor of the Israelites. Leading God's people is one of the most humbling experiences. It is worth the double reward that the Bible promises. The Bible says that pastors have double reward but also double judgment. In the dry season obeying God can determine our destiny. Some pastors are wondering why they cannot seem to get to the promise land. The promise land could be where the church is experiencing new members and ministries are being effective in the local community. In some cases, churches aren't entering into their promise land could be because pastors have failed to do what God has commanded during their dry season. The devil wants nothing better than for us to fall short of the anointing that God has in store for us. He will do whatever it takes. He wants us to grow frustrated in our dry season and act against God's word in frustration. If we have to settle for seeing our promises from a far off, Satan feels as though he has won. Do not become frustrated like Moses, but stand on your faith. When you do not feel powerful and when you do not sense God's power, bind the enemy anyhow. Our faith is the greatest tool during the dry season because we can call on those things we do not see or feel. Dry seasons are very active in the spirit realm. In dry seasons, Christians become weary and easily influenced. I end this chapter with a commandment of the apostle Paul, "When you have done all you can do to stand, stand!" Even if you're weary, stand anyway. When you are tired and drained, continue by faith call in your strength and restoration.

Chapter 14
Drenched Trench

"Thus says the Lord: 'Make this valley full of ditches.' [17] For thus says the Lord: 'You shall not see wind, nor shall you see rain; yet that valley shall be filled with water, so that you, your cattle, and your animals may drink.'
2Kings3:16

The very thing that defines a dry season is water. The only thing that keeps a place dry is water or the lack thereof. Earlier in the book I told you about a young lady who experienced a dry season and allowed the frustration of the dry season to run her back to her previous sinful lifestyle. The young lady thought the presence of God left because she wasn't praying long enough, so she decided to pray twice as long. The young lady then thought that if she read her Bible more, her frustration and stale feelings would disappear. She started reading her Bible twice as much without getting the results she anticipated. The lady even got to the place where she blamed the church because she did not feel God during the corporate church setting. She could not understand why reading her Bible, praying twice as long, and going to church did not suffice her feelings of being plain ole' dry. If I had the opportunity to go back in time and explain to her about dry seasons, I would tell her reading the Bible is necessary. I would explain to her that praying is essential. I would enlighten her that going to church is vital. I would then teach her that there is nothing you can do to get yourself out of a dry season. You can pray, you can go to church every time the doors are open, and you can read the Bible from cover to cover, but you do not determine when you get out of a dry season. The reality is God led you to the dry season. God is the only one who can get you out. In a dry season, you cannot provide yourself with water or else you wouldn't truly be in a dry season. Why do Christians think that if they pray harder, go to church more that they could lead themselves out of a dry season? God leads you into a dry season, and God leads you out of them. It is solely on God. Whenever God decides that he wants to speak again then he will. We find ourselves often trying to buy God's presence with our works. The lady that became frustrated and turned her back on God had this mindset. It is the mindset of I am working God, but you aren't paying me. When we work a job, we expect to get paid for our work. If we consistently work and do not get paid from the owner then we quit. This thinking is the same thinking that drove many Christians to walk away from God .God does not operate in this way. We cannot buy or manipulate God. God does not pay us according to how much we pray. We cannot back God into a corner and show Him the list of all our works. God does not pay us according to our works. What moves God is our faith and our obedience. Our works cannot get us out of a dry season, but they do play a part. When you are going through a dry season there is only two things that you should do. The first thing that you should do is embrace it. James 1:2-4 *My brethren, count it all joy when you fall into various trials, ³ knowing that the testing of your faith produces patience. ⁴ But let patience have its perfect work, that you may be perfect and complete, lacking nothing.*" When you go through a dry season instead of fighting it the whole time, why don't you try embracing the season. James says that we should count it joy when our faith is tested because when our faith is tested it produces patience. There is that dreaded word again patience. When you are patient, you are not anxious or worried. Patience goes hand and hand with peace. Even in a dry season, you can still have peace. Dry seasons do not have to be as anxious and painful as we make them out to be. The key word is "as" anxious and as painful. Dry seasons will always have an element of pain because God is cutting away flesh. Dry seasons are hard and tedious, but mostly because we do not have peace. We must first possess peace before our dry season is peaceful. We can speak to our minds and the storms of the dry season and command them to be peaceful. The disciples were in the middle of water. Suddenly a storm came and the winds and waves caused the disciples to panic. Jesus spoke to the circumstances and told the wind and waves to be peaceful. Jesus spoke peace because he had peace. Jesus had to first have peace before he could give it away. How do we know Jesus had peace? We know Jesus had peace because while the disciples where running frantic, Jesus was at the bottom of the boat asleep. The circumstances did not affect Jesus. We cannot let the dry season steal our peace. Without peace during the dry seasons in our life, we will look at the surroundings and give up. Even with peace, dry seasons are tough. James goes on to say that when we embrace the testing of our faith; it stretches us and matures us to be perfect and complete. It is remarkable and insightful at what this scripture is truly saying. It is challenging us as Christians to have a future based mindset. We need to look passed our current circumstances and dry feelings. We should embrace the dry season because if we look in the near future this dry season and test from God will eventually allow God to promote me because he can trust me with the little things. The little things like obeying his voice when he is not looking over my shoulders. The little things like remembering the commands he has told us. Having integrity that even when I feel God is not present, I will still do what is right in His sight. If God can trust you with the little things, he will promote you to greater things. Everyone wants to do incredibly things for God, but if God cannot trust you to obey his word when there are five people in the congregation, what makes you think that he will trust you with three thousand. We must embrace the dry season. Fighting and dreading the dry season only exhausts us more. Embrace the season look to the future because it will only make you a stronger Christian. The first thing that we should do during our dry season is embrace it. The next thing that we should do is dig!

Some may be wondering, what in the world am I talking about digging? It is a good question. A question I may have asked if I was in your shoes. What does digging have to do with me being in the most painful growing season of my spiritual life? It has everything to do with it.

Digging is the key to your breakthrough. Digging is an action you must take. 2 Kings 3:1-18 tells and unbelievable story. The story goes like this. The nation of Israel had been split into two nations. Yes you could call it a church split. In the north was the nation of Israel. The nation of Israel was the bigger of the two. South of Israel was the nation of Judah. Jehoram became the king of Israel. The nations that Israel had subdued and beaten in war were no longer afraid of Israel because Jehoram was now king. It is kind of like the substitute teacher coming in and all the kids taking advantage of her. I remember in my life B.C. (before Christ) of course, my classmates and I gave substitute teachers fits. I must admit it was not all my fault, she asked for it on this occasion. The teacher was middle aged and very grumpy. She came in and was very abrasive. My classmates and I were not used to this because our normal teacher was very sweet. After a couple of hours of her trying to prove she had authority, the class went into a complete uproar. It all started with her tripping and falling in front of the class. The class erupted in laughter. This, however; was just the beginning. As she is falling to the carpet in the classroom something changes. Our substitute teacher looks different. There is something about her that looks strange. Her wig had fallen off. Talk about bad luck. As the teacher is sitting on the floor with her wig in her hand, I remember thinking that this is so sad and embarrassing. I do what any other responsible kid would do. I look at the wig again and begin to laugh to the point of tears. Of course this was not the proper way to handle the situation, but that does not stop it from being funny. Now back to the story. After Jehoram parents died, the nation of Moab no longer wanted to pay Israel the sheep and wool that it was accustomed to paying Israel under Jehoram's parents. Jehoram, like the substitute teacher, decides he will not tolerate Moab's rebellion. Jehoram decided to make an alliance with the nation of Judah and Edom. The two other kings agree to help Israel. All three kings meet up and head towards Moab. The Bible says that they decided to go through the desert of Edom and ran out of water. Here we go again. Another dry season and another place where there is no water. The three kings were stuck in a desert with three huge armies and animals, and they had no water. While they are thirsting away in the desert, someone came up with the great idea to call for the man of God. Elisha unenthusiastically answers the call of King Jehoram. Elisha finds the three kings in a desert with no water. Elisha says if it was not for the king of Judah he would have never answered the call of King Jehoram.

Here is a brief point, your friends matter. Your friends and who you travel with can cause God to show up in your life. When Elisha shows up, the people beg Elisha to give them a word regarding their dry season. The people were expecting God to tell them where to find water. I can imagine the King of Israel wanting God to provide an immediate way out of the desert. Elisha calls on his worship team. The worship team begins to set the mood for Elisha to pray. Elisha listens to the strings of the harp and hears what God is saying. God says something peculiar. God doesn't tell the people where the underground well stored with water is. The prophet doesn't come to the rescue with gallons of water to help the nations. The prophet tells the people to dig ditches. The Lord said through the prophet to dig, and God will provide the rest. It would not be through wind or rain, but it would be a supernatural work of God. God did not want it to be through wind or rain because then the people would count it as coincidence. God wanted to make sure the people knew that this was a supernatural miracle from God. The Israelites dug valleys and when they woke, there was enough water for not only the men in the camp but enough water for their animals to. What do you mean by dig? How do I dig? Well I'm glad you asked. When we are in our dry seasons, Christians make the mistake of thinking that digging is their source of water. Reading the bible, praying, and going to church all of those things are the digging. The young lady who eventual got frustrated in her dry season thought that the digging was her source of strength. It is not. Water is the only source during a dry season. If you rely on your digging then you will get worn out. The digging is not the thing giving you the water. The digging only allows a way for the water to be captured. If the Israelites had not dug ditches, they would not have had any way to capture the water that God would eventual send. When we pray, we are digging a ditch. When we attend church, we are digging a ditch. When we read our Bible, we are digging a ditch. We are making ways so when the water is released; we have a way to capture it. God supplies the water. Our digging the ditch does not have any influence on when God sends the water. Do not get into thinking that digging the ditch is your source. God is your source. Digging those trenches only helps capture the rain God will bring. My last dry season I read my bible every night, and I continued to pray. This went on for about two months. It was a Saturday night, and I was reading my Bible. Like the past two months, it felt dry. It just didn't seem like I was reading the word of God .I did not feel anything what so ever. The next day I get up and drag myself out of bed. I had to force myself to go to church because I did not want to witness other people experiencing God while I had to settle for being dry. Even though it was tough, I forced my way to church. It felt like the same old story through the first three worship songs. I was singing words on a projector, but the words had no feelings behind them. It felt as if I had been in a fifteen round title fight. The third song was coming to a close, and the worship team transitioned to the fourth song. Suddenly when the fourth song began to play, I heard God speak to me about a scripture that I had read the night before. God's voice sent chills down my spine. His voice entering into my ears lifted a weight off of my shoulders. God was speaking to me again. I was out of my dry season. He began to affirm me. He began telling me that he never left my side. He reassured me that He has a greater plan. Tears began to stream down my face. I could not hold back my emotions. I was out of the desert. God had given me water. God just by speaking replenished my spirit. I dug a ditch by reading the Bible the night before. I dug a ditch by forcing myself to go to church. If I had not read the scripture the night before or if I had not attend church the morning after, God would have no ditch to fill up in my life. The ditches that I dug allowed God to spring up water into my dry season. If I had not dug that ditch then I would have had no way to retain the water that God was pouring out. When we dig, we create a trench. The trench is not our substance. It is not our source of fulfillment, but it gives a place when God is ready to fill our trenches with water. When we build that trench, we are giving ourselves opportunities to get ourselves out of the dry season. Do not fail to realize that the digging isn't the source. You never know how close you are to having water supplied. You may have been reading your Bible for 6 months and feel nothing. Do not give up because your dry season could be closer than you expect.

Closer Than You Think

"Then God opened her eyes and she saw a well of water. So she went and filled the skin with water and gave the boy a drink." Genesis 21:19

Hagar the maidservant of Abraham was casted out of the house by Sarah, Abraham's wife. Talk about putting Abraham in a bad position. Sarah didn't believe God and forced her husband to conceive a child by Hagar. Hagar has a child and now Sarah finds out she is pregnant. Poor Abraham talk about being stuck between a rock and a hard place. Sarah talks Abraham into kicking Ishmael and Hagar out of the house. Abraham gave them a loaf of bread and a canteen of water. After walking and drinking all the water, Hagar finds herself in a desert with her son Ishmael. When they were all out of water, Hagar was giving up faith. She laid her son underneath a bush because she couldn't watch her son die. Suddenly an angel of the Lord came to Hagar in the desert. The Bible says that God opened her eyes so that she could see a well of water. The well had been there the whole time. Hagar had not realized how close to her breakthrough she was. When she was giving up hope, God gave her insight about her dry season. Do not give up hope. You do not realize how close to your breakthrough you are. You may not see the light at the end of the tunnel, but God can open your eyes. Just like Hagar you never know how close you are to your dry season ending. The whole time Hagar was just a few steps away from her well of resource. Dry seasons sometimes cause us not to see clearly. We should never give up. We should never turn our backs. We never know when God will open our eyes and show us the well of water.

Living Water

Jesus approached a Samaritan woman who was minding her own business. This woman was at a well trying to obtain water. Jesus asks her for a drink and she is slightly confused because Jesus is a Jew, and she is a Samaritan. The woman does not realize that Jesus is baiting her, and she is about to receive some of the deepest revelation on worship in the New Testament. Jesus tells her, if you knew who you were talking to, you would have asked me for water. The woman is still thinking in the natural. Jesus is talking supernatural. Jesus is referring to the Holy Spirit. The Holy Spirit is the key to your dry season. The Holy Spirit is water to the souls of men. He refreshes and gives nourishment. The Holy Spirit is God. Jesus said whoever believes in me streams of living water will flow from within them. God the Holy Spirit is our source. In our dry season when we are under spiritual attack embrace it because where there is water there is substance. Demons can't function where the Living Water is. Why is it that demons search arid places when evicted? It is because water in the natural represents the Holy Spirit in the supernatural. The enemy wants to stay far away from the Holy Spirit. Wherever the Holy Spirit is there is always light and can be no darkness. When we are underneath spiritual attack during our dry season, remember that you have a river of Living Water. You are never actually dry. You have the Holy Spirit inside of you. Though it feels dry and it feels stale. The river that is inside of you is flowing and not stagnant.

Arise the Winter is Past

"My beloved spoke, and said to me, Rise up, my love, my fair one, and come away. For lo, the winter is past...' Song of Solomon 2:10-11

Seasons are like book chapters. They always come to an end. When we are stuck in our dry season, it feels as if it will last forever. Let's not get into the mistake of making the dry season more than what it is. Yes, they are a struggle. On the other hand, they are our weight building exercises. Dry seasons make us stronger. They build character and make us a scary opponent for the enemy. When we go to the gym and workout, it doesn't always feel comfortable. In the immediate days after, your muscles actually hurt, but we know that they hurt because they are getting stronger. When we are in the dry season and it hurts to pray because you don't feel like God is listening, remember your struggle is making you stronger. Let's keep the dry season in proper context. Even though it may hurt, it is only because it is building faith inside of us. In the middle of your dry season, it feels like one day is equivalent to a month. We must not make it more than what it is. A dry season is still a season. Every season comes to an end. Remember this too shall past. In Song of

Solomon this is the very thing that is taking place. There is a waking process that the author of Song of Solomon is telling his loved one that the winter is over and the storms of the dry season are over. You may be experiencing staleness. You may miss those times when God feels near to you, but do not worry. Your season is coming to an end. God is going to awaken you and tell you to arise. God is about to tell you that your winter has pasted. As the writer of this book, I will speak prophetically by the Spirit. Your season is coming to an end. Your long hard harsh winter where things usually die is coming to a halt. The reason why the winter has hurt so much was because God was cutting on you. God loves you so much that He won't let you stay the same. He has been cutting away some flesh and allowing some of those weeds to die off. Soon and very soon, God is about to tell you to arise. He is about to change the season in your life. The dryness is about to be swallowed up with rivers of living waters. You are about to start blossoming. The reason your winter was so harsh is because the promise land is near. God is making you into a quick study. The place that God is bringing you, will need you to have faith to change lives. God is about to blossom you into a radical lover of Him. The type of radical that whether you feel Him or not, you are always pursuing. God put you through this season to build your faith. Faith only comes from being thrown into the fire and being refined. God is building an army of believers that operate in faith to change cultures. He is looking to America. When homosexuality, drugs, and sex run rampant, God wants people who won't be discouraged by the surroundings because they see through the eyes of faith. It is in the dry season that we can truly build faith that calls things that are not as though they are. I believe you are about to have your greatest harvest yet. Not because you are more anointed, but because you endured your dry season and allowed God to kill your flesh.

Dry seasons are a part of life. It is totally up to us to trust God and allow him to perfect us. The dry seasons are our spiritual test in life. How we handle those test determines if God can promote us or not. The good news is that if we hold firm to His word there is special blessings and anointings awaiting us. Isaiah 55:6 says seek the Lord while he may be found. The implication is there will come a time where God hides himself and we will not be able to find him. Hebrews 11:6 says that God rewards those who earnestly seek Him. The only time someone seeks something is when they can no longer find it. When we diligently seek God, there are rewards for us. God leads us to the dry seasons of our lives. It is in these dry seasons that boys become men and girls become women. Even though you feel unproductive, there are a lot of things going on in the heavens. You are under the most attack spiritual because your dry season goes hand and hand with your destiny. Do not make the mistake of Moses and disobey God's voice in your dry season. Follow the example of Christ who stood on the word of God to get him though his dry season. Remember to dig trenches and allow the Holy Spirit room to rain down in your life. Embrace your dry season. Your dry season is still a season. Like all seasons, they come to an end. You may be closer to finishing your test than you realize.

About the Author

God has given Pastor Rontrell Edwards a burning desire to reach this generation. He believes teens and young adults are searching for the truth, but are force fed temporary satisfaction by Hollywood. Rontrell Edwards believes that we are living in the last days and there is a generation arising that will live out Heaven on Earth. Signs and wonders will follow this generation because they are occupied only with Jesus. Pastor Rontrell's heart is to preach a relevant word, disciple this generation, and create an environment where young people can practice what they hear preached. His heart is to awaken America by the Power of the Holy Spirit. He longs to see revival break out amongst the dead and sleeping. That Christians will rise up with boldness and fire and reach a dead dying world. Pastor Edwards has traveled to multiple states and has seen the power of God transform people. He has witnessed drug addicts radically set free without withdrawals. He has seen altars filled with teenagers who are tired of settling for the world's wisdom. These same teenagers become love sick for their Lord Jesus. The heart of Pastor Edwards is to turn the hearts of a generation back to their creator.

To Contact Pastor Rontrell for a Speaking Engagement email him at: edwardsrontrell@gmail.com or rontrell44@aol.com

Follow Pastor Rontrell on Twitter @rontrelledwards